WHY ARE THE JAPANESE NON-RELIGIOUS?

Japanese Spirituality:
Being Non-Religious in a Religious Culture

Toshimaro Ama

University Press of America,® Inc.
Lanham · Boulder · New York · Toronto · Oxford

Copyright © 2005 by
University Press of America,® Inc.
4501 Forbes Boulevard
Suite 200
Lanham, Maryland 20706
UPA Acquisitions Department (301) 459-3366

PO Box 317
Oxford
OX2 9RU, UK

All rights reserved
Printed in the United States of America
British Library Cataloging in Publication Information Available

Library of Congress Control Number: 2004114183
ISBN 0-7618-3056-1 (paperback : alk. ppr.)

♾™ The paper used in this publication meets the minimum
requirements of American National Standard for Information
Sciences—Permanence of Paper for Printed Library Materials,
ANSI Z39.48—1984

Contents

Foreword

Ama, Toshimaro is widely acknowledged in Japan as a leading scholar of Japanese religions in the modern and contemporary periods. His questions about the nature of religion in general, and Japanese religion in particular, have offered a model for understanding how the Japanese case illuminates works of religiosity, especially in modernity and beyond.

This translation of his landmark 1996 *Why Are the Japanese Non-Religious? Japanese Spirituality: Being Non-Religious in a Religious Culture* is the first attempt to offer Ama's analysis to a broader English-speaking audience. One of the reasons that this book attracted so much attention in Japan is the style of writing that sums up a broad range of scholarly literature in an easy-to-read manner, accompanied by insightful analysis. Seamlessly examining Buddhism, Shinto, Christianity, folk religion, and religion in the public sphere, this work will be of tremendous value to both students of religion and contemporary Japan.

Duncan Ryūken Williams
University of California, Irvine

Preface

Why Are the Japanese Non-Religious? *Japanese Spirituality: Being Non-Religious in a Religious Culture* (Original Japanese title: *Nihonjin wa naze mushūkyō nanoka*), written by Ama, Toshimaro, Professor at Meiji Gakuin University in Tokyo, was first published by Chikuma shobō in 1996 and has since sold more than 100,000 copies in Japan. The book has been read as a text by many university students in the fields of both Japanese cultural and ethnic research and religious studies. Various intellectuals have also taken an interest in its contents, as well the public in general, which has become concerned with its own religious identity.

This book was translated into Korean and published by Yemoonseowon in South Korea in 2000 and will be soon published in German. This, however, is the first attempt to translate it into English.

The book explains how folklore and culture have been integrated into the Japanese religious mind. In Japan, religion is still defined in the Western sense, in which Christianity remains dominant. The Japanese on the whole avoid or lack an understanding of organized religions, yet at the same time, when asked about their own religious beliefs, many Japanese are unable to respond, as they are unsure of these in themselves. For Japanese, Shinto, Christianity, and Buddhism are all mixed together; as a child, one is taken to Shinto shrines and as an adult, one attends both chapel weddings and Buddhist funerals. Therefore, Japanese think that they do not need to be committed to any particular religion. In a sense, this is *mushūkyō*, which literally means "a lack of religious beliefs." *Shūkyō* is a word created in the Meiji period (1868-1912) as the translation for "religion," which referred to organized belief in the European sense, while *mu* literally means not existing. However, the majority of Japanese people have never examined the concept of *mushūkyō* very carefully; this book examines why they have avoided participating in organized religion. The author was motivated to analyze the Japanese religious mind for if its development is not clearly defined soon, Japanese spiritual life will disappear completely someday.

In this book, the author has classified Japanese religion into two groups: revealed religion (Christianity as well as Buddhism) and natural religion.[1] When a Japanese person says that he/she is non-religious, it refers to the former type; the latter type is seen as ancestor worship, which has never been organized because it does not contain a particular set of doctrines, though it has been the center of many Japanese activities.

In Chapter 1, the author introduces examples of ways in which the majority of Japanese lack religious belief. While describing their customary practices of observing *hatsumōde* and *obon*, the author examines the popular religious events in Japan. Then, through cases of Constitutional litigation, the author analyzes ways that Japanese intellectuals understand religion. Chapter 2 discusses the development of the Japanese religious mind up to the beginning of the Meiji period, roughly between the late twelfth and mid nineteenth century. Between the late twelfth and fourteenth century the question of afterlife was a serious concern. As the wheel of rebirth dictated the Japanese believe in the physical existence of hell and Amida Buddha's Pure Land, the promise of escaping from such fears and from one's sufferings urged people to seek spiritual liberation. Nevertheless, this activity stopped once the Japanese became more confident with economic growth, which turned attention away from the matter of afterlife and toward the satisfaction of present life. In this environment, Confucianism played an important role as a guideline for human relationships. In Chapter 3, the development of the religious mind in the Meiji period is presented. Up to the end of World War II, this was strictly controlled by the state, which fostered Shinto in order to strengthen Emperor worship. As a result, religion was divided into two spheres: personal belief and social conduct. Personal belief was guaranteed under freedom of religion, as outlined in the Constitution of the Empire of Japan (though this was still conditional). Social conduct, or the expression of personal belief, was strictly prohibited as a threat to nationalism. By law, therefore, only the former was officially acknowledged, and this has become the recognized definition of religion today. The author explains how both revealed and natural religions were changed for the worse in this period. In Chapter 4, the cultural and ethnic influences of natural religion are introduced through the ideas of Yanagita Kunio (1875-1962), leader of the Japanese folklore study group.

Japanese culture has always emphasized harmony in the community, which Yanagita calls the "value of just being ordinary," and it has always rejected extraordinary individual talent, no matter how excellent it might be. As a result, three religions, Shinto, Confucianism, and especially Buddhism were similar in that each was adapted in its own way to suit Japan. In other words, both revealed and natural religions have become secularized since the seventeenth century. In Chapter 5, however, the author examines two examples of spiritually-enriched lives from both categories which have opposed the stance of *mushūkyō*: one is the traditional life of Shin Buddhism, or Jōdoshinshū, followers; the other is that of the people of Okinawa.

This English translation will hopefully contribute to the history of Japan's religious development and be useful to those in the United States as well as in Europe who are studying Japanese religion or are interested in this particular field of study.

Ama, Michihiro
June 2004

1. The original Japanese for "revealed religion" is *soshō shūkyō,* and that for "natural religion" is *shizen shūkyō.* Revealed religion indicates organized religion whereas natural religion can be replaced with folklore religion. Nevertheless, the author's purpose is to discern the origin of these two, as revealed religion is advocated by particular groups, while natural religion is formed rather "naturally" as mores and integrated gradually into the lives of communities.

Translator's Notes

In this translation, Japanese words are written in italic, except for recognized words or titles such as Tokyo, Shinto, kami, and Tokugawa shogunate, as well as people's names, temples, and geographical areas. When referring to Japanese personal names, the family name appears first, according to custom.

I would like to thank Dr. Dennis Hirota for guidance, Rev. and Mrs. Peter Lait for guidance and advice, Dr. Duncan Williams for writing Foreword, Dr. Alfred Bloom for making a title suggestion, Ms. Anna Ress Campbell for editing, and my wife Tomoko for arranging maps and personal support.

Ama, Michihiro

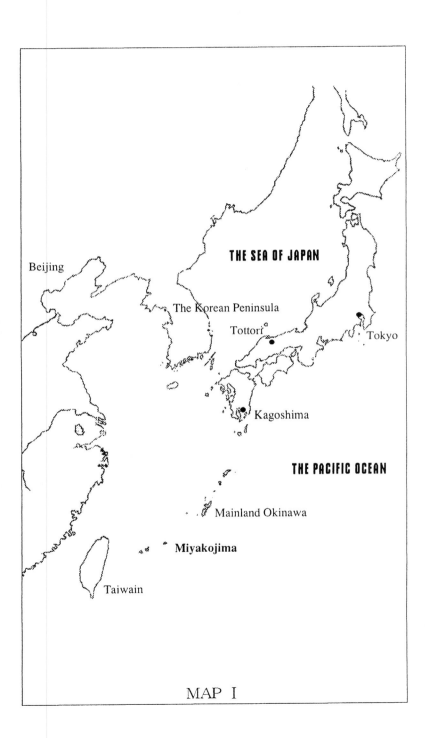

THE SEA OF JAPAN

Beijing

The Korean Peninsula

Tottori

Tokyo

Kagoshima

THE PACIFIC OCEAN

Mainland Okinawa

Miyakojima

Taiwain

MAP I

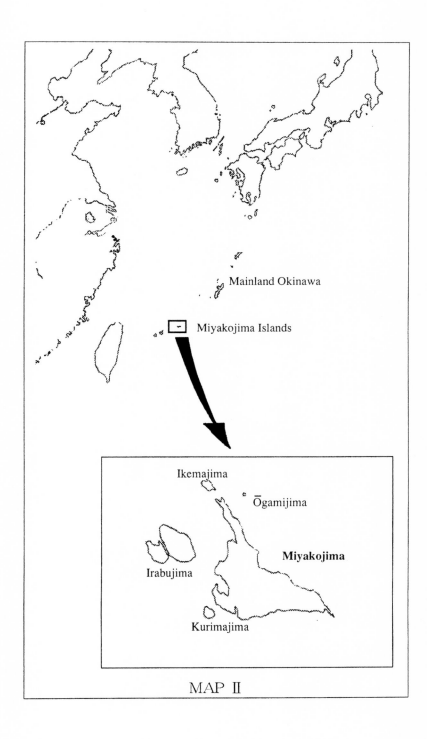

Mainland Okinawa

Miyakojima Islands

Ikemajima

Ōgamijima

Miyakojima

Irabujima

Kurimajima

MAP II

Chapter 1

What Does it Mean to "Lack Religious Beliefs" (*mushūkyō*)?

1. Revealed Religion versus Natural Religion

Many people in Japan see themselves as non-religious, even though only a few genuinely reject the actual value of religion or are in fact atheists. This is clearly shown in surveys on Japanese attitudes toward religion. At the same time, however, of those who say they are non-religious, about seventy-five percent feel that a religious attitude is important. In other words, more than half the people surveyed felt that though they were personally non-religious, being religious was an important quality. What can we make of all this? I think the secret behind this personal lack of religious belief, may be found in the Japanese responses themselves.[1]

When most Japanese say that they are non-religious they do not mean they are atheists, but rather that they are not affiliated with any particular religious denomination. Indeed, they possess a rich religious sensibility, but they resist limiting their religious feelings to one particular teaching. For example, when purchasing cemetery plots, most Japanese do not wish to be asked with which Buddhist denomination they are affiliated, even though they may visit the graves afterwards to offer flowers and food and ask Buddhist priests to chant sutras over them. It is as though they do not consider these activities religious. Another example is the funeral ceremony itself, held often without Buddhist clergy. Non-religious mourners put flowers into the coffin, play music, and read poems in order to bring back memories of the deceased. In addition, they try to console themselves with the belief that death means returning to the earth, or that the elements of the physical body combine together in other forms later on. In my opinion, these activities are quite religious in outlook, for they seek to find a meaning in life in order to accept death.

When I read an autobiography of a local Shinto priest (*kannushi*), I was surprised to find that the author, Kanzaki Nobutake, identified himself as a person of no religious belief. According to Kanzaki, the position was hereditary, and in becoming a priest he had fulfilled community expectations, since he was only needed for local festivals. It was, therefore, unnecessary for him to be faithful to deities, and he concluded by saying that as his community did not require a certain set of Shinto beliefs, he could perform his work even though he was not religious. While sympathetic toward his efforts to serve as a Shinto priest simultaneously carrying on another occupation, I was surprised at his unquestioning (though honest) assumption that the feelings of the local people should be labeled as non-religious including himself. His attitude reflects the religious consciousness of the majority of Japanese nowadays. If religion is understood based on the model of Christianity, then the indigenous festivals (*matsuri*) associated with Shinto cannot be accepted as religious.

When overseas trips first became popular for Japanese, many guidebooks cautioned travelers against identifying themselves as non-religious, since being seen as an atheist could make a bad impression. Although it was recommended to declare oneself a Buddhist or Shinto follower, many Japanese were unable to explain the religion when asked to do so, as they were no longer sure of their religious identity, even if they regarded themselves as non-religious.

As more and more Japanese students continue traveling and studying overseas nowadays, many continue to have this kind of experience. For example, when one of my students visited the United States for a short period and identified himself as non-religious, many people were concerned about his not being able to develop as a person. After coming back, he became uncomfortable with his lack of religious understanding and decided to take my class; this student eventually wrote a graduation thesis on Japanese religious feelings. I have observed many similar cases and therefore believe that identifying oneself as non-religious needs to be understood from a Japanese perspective.

Since the Japanese religious mind is rather complex, it cannot be easily compared with Christianity or Islam; misunderstanding often occurs due to the confusion between revealed and natural religion. Examples of revealed religions include Christianity, Buddhism, Islam, and Japanese new religions, which are revealed through texts, preached about by certain people, and managed by profitable organizations. By contrast, it is hard to define natural religion or to ascertain precisely when it emerged, who preached about it, or how it was adopted into the lives of the people. It was established in communities and gradually spread over the region as time passed, though there was no prevailing sense of propagation. If the Japanese who go overseas understand their non-religious identity as merely a lack of belief in revealed religion rather than natural religion, they might become more confident. Unfortunately, such an understanding has, in general, not grown very much.

2. The Religious Feeling of the Non-Religious

Being non-religious means a rejection of revealed religion but imply an identification with natural religion. *Hatsumōde*, the first visit to shrines and temples during the New Year holidays, and *obon*, the Buddhist custom of honoring ancestral spirits in late summer, are both good examples for the analysis of the Japanese religious mind. At the beginning of January 1996, over eighty million people visited shrines and temples, including both the young, who seldom visit shrines at other times of the year, and the elderly, who go to pray for happiness and success in the coming year. Public transportation operates twenty-four hours a day during the first few days of January, when shrine and temple areas are crowded with worshipers. Although news media routinely report upon the busiest shrines and temples in terms of monetary donations and number of visitors, the religious identity of those visitors is hardly discussed publicly. It is as if *hatsumōde* is one more event that occurs during holiday seasons.

Obon is observed from the thirteenth to fifteenth of either

July or August. Since many people return to their home towns, public transportation is overcrowded and those who try to avoid it end up in heavy traffic. Why do these people want to go home, knowing what they will have to put up with on the way? It is because both *hatsumōde* and *obon* are the most important times for family gatherings, at which ancestral spirits are believed to return. These customs are the signs of the Japanese religious mind, which I identify as natural religion, although Japanese individuals themselves may not make this distinction. Natural religion, in this case, is a matter of worshiping one's ancestors and the tutelary deity of one's community (*chinju no kami* or *ujigami*). Traditionally, the Japanese believe that after a person dies, his or her spirit eventually becomes a deity (*kami*) that will protect the family; the memorial service becomes an important means of honoring the deceased. In addition, many Japanese believe in the reincarnation of the spirit and that a newborn baby is the rebirth of a deceased ancestor. Or they may believe that the spirit remains on a nearby mountain or in a forest, watching over them. *Higan* or *ohigan* (the other shore), which is held at the vernal and autumnal equinoxes, is a ritual to transfer the deceased spirit from this world to the other, in which people visiting a cemetery slowly pour water onto their ancestors' grave. According to Yanagita Kunio (1875-1962), a pioneer in the study of Japanese folklore, this water must be drawn from the same well that was used for the person's first bath as a baby. This ritual represents the family's sympathy for the deceased; the spirit of the deceased lives with the family. After Buddhism was introduced into Japan, people yearned for birth in the Pure Land, where one could enjoy a peaceful afterlife. This belief, however, imparted a sense of remoteness from the deceased; for this reason, people needed some kind of ritual to comfort themselves. As the Japanese started making graves only in the eighteenth century, this custom is relatively recent and is not found in any other country.

Since the annual festivals of *hatsumōde, obon,* and *higan* were means of obtaining peace of mind, there was no need for people to choose revealed religion as their declared means of spiritual liberation.

3. Is Christmas a Religious Festival?

The majority of Japanese do not regard rituals as part of religious activities but rather see them as customs. For instance, while Christmas is a holy day for Christians, sutra chanting is important in Buddhist funerals, and ground-breaking ceremony is necessary for Shinto, these practices have become merely customs for many people. Even those who do not consider themselves Christians enjoy Christmas parties as year-end events, and many do not hesitate to attend Shinto weddings or Buddhist funerals. At the same time, some of those who have faith in revealed religions do not observe these events very religiously. Either way, such events are not seen as religious, which raises some questions: Why and how are rituals separated from religion itself, and why is the customary practice of the rituals not considered religion?

Before analyzing this through the history of Japan's modernization, I would like to give some more examples of the complexity of the Japanese religious mind. In 1995, I visited a village called Higashi Shirakawa, located in Gifu prefecture, where the movement to "abolish Buddha and destroy Śākyamuni" (*haibutsu kishaku*) entitled a suppression of Buddhism and the removal of all Buddhist influence from Shinto. This movement was very strong in the late nineteenth century, when the Meiji government (1868-1912) centralized Japan by sanctifying the Emperor. Shinto ideology prevailed at that time, calling for the removal of any Buddhist influence from the area; thus, many temples and statues were destroyed. Buddhist monks were also forced to return to lay life. Even today, a stone monument upon which the six letters of Namu-Amida-Butsu are inscribed, and which was broken into four pieces during the nineteenth century, can be found in front of the Higashi Shirakawa village. The villagers identified themselves as non-religious, even though a Shinto altar was placed in each household to honor the tutelary deity in their community (*ujigami*) and various other deities (*kamigami*). Shinto-style funerals were also performed there and the villagers believed that the spirits of the deceased would become deities. This phenomenon suggests that there was strong manipulation on the part of the Meiji government, which I will discuss in Chapter 3.

In my opinion, Shinto is derived from natural religion but is not a natural religion itself. Shinto developed as a belief system in the Court in which the Emperor was apotheosized, and it appeared as early as the ninth century. Shinto's belief in kami is preserved through natural religion and reconstructed by Chinese philosophy, among other influences. Although the founder of Shinto is unknown, the religion has been formalized since the ninth century. Shinto can be classified somewhere between revealed and natural religion.

4. Is the Ground-Breaking Ceremony Religious?

Although every religion has its own roots, it is difficult to determine the origin of natural religion in Japan because its rituals have become custom, and the separation of religion and politics, guaranteed under the Constitution, is now controversial. For instance, local authorities sponsor the Festival of Offering Rice (*kenkokusai*), in which harvested rice is offered to the kami in preparation for the Festival of New-Tasting (*ninamesai*) which takes place at the Imperial Palace in the autumn. Since public funds were spent on the Festival of Offering Rice, some people debated whether this violated the Constitution. The court decided that the festival had nothing to do with religion, as it was quite natural, and in October 1993, public expenditure for the festival was deemed legal.

The precedent for the 1993 case was the Constitutional litigation of Tsu's ground-breaking ceremony (*jichinsai*) in the capital city of Mie prefecture. In 1965, before construction of a public gymnasium began, the city had a Shinto ground-breaking ceremony. The litigation, which took a total of twelve years, began at the local district court, ending eventually in the Supreme Court. In the first decision, this ceremony was recognized as legal because there was no intention to propagate Shinto, and many people were already accustomed to such ceremonies. In the second court, however, the first judgment was overturned with the ruling that "religious activities" should have been defined more carefully. Not only should individual teachings, festivals, and ceremonies have been discussed, but the effect of propagation through rituals should have been examined as well. The second judgment interpreted the separation of religion and politics statute as a prohibition of government assistance for any kind of activity expressing religious sentiment. Nevertheless, the Supreme Court ruled against this second decision. Although the ceremony itself was Shinto in nature and quite religious, it was hard to imagine that the ceremony would disturb people by forcing Shinto values upon them. The understanding of the judges was that once religion was secularized (i.e., rituals became merely customs), it was no longer regarded as religion. The judges were also strongly prejudiced against ordinary people, presuming they were too ignorant to discuss the separation of religion and politics as their religious feelings were a combination of both Shinto and Buddhism.

Another example is Yasukuni Shrine, located in the Kudan district of Chiyoda ward, Tokyo, which enshrines those people who sacrificed their lives for Japan from the beginning of the Meiji period to the end of World War II in 1945. Although official support for the shrine ceased upon Japan's defeat, appeals for its recovery have been growing stronger, which suggests the threat of Japan's possible re-militarization both domestically and internationally. When such a bill was debated in parliament, some Liberal Democratic Party (LDP) Diet members made statements that freedom of religion had been designed for Christians alone and worship of kami should be seen merely as a normal practice for most Japanese. It was clear that for these LDP members, religion meant revealed religion, particularly Christianity.

At the funeral of the late Emperor Shōwa (1901-1989), both private and public services were observed. Although the private services were held in Shinto style and the public services were supposed to be free from any religious acts, it was difficult to draw the line between the two; participating in both ceremonies were numerous government officials including the Prime Minister, Diet, Cabinet, and Judicial members, and ten thousand public attendees. The question concerning a possible violation of the Constitution was highly debated. Some people argued that the funeral should have been observed as a national event and that the public performance of Shinto rituals would not violate the Constitution. According to Mayuzumi Toshirō, the essence of Shōwa's funeral was lost without the public observance of Shinto rituals.

When the next emperor was inaugurated at the Festival of the Great Food Offering (*daijōsai*), the same issue was brought up again, while the government continued hosting Shinto ceremonies.

One may often watch seasonal Shinto festivals on television; however, it seems that only a few people wonder whether broadcasting companies are paid to do so or whether they simply privatize the air waves. The broadcasting companies are not careful about this issue, because the separation of ritual from religion is widely accepted in society.

5. Is Being Religious Strange?

It seems that incidents and scandals surrounding religious organizations further contribute to the unpopularity of revealed religion. For instance, some groups are reported to have deceived their members into making large donations, performed supernatural events, or brainwashed members. Mystical practices carried out by such organizations seem out of place, and since they exceed one's knowledge and experience, the majority of Japanese feel uncomfortable with them. On the other hand, respectful of community harmony, many are comfortable with the worship of ancestral spirits and their community's tutelary deities because they never threaten their interests.

Walking down a busy street in Ginza, Tokyo, on any afternoon, one may hear a few Christians aimlessly calling for confessions of one's sins and for repentance. Passers-by are oblivious to the message as they believe themselves to be good people, and instead look down on these preachers for disturbing the peace with their loudspeakers. Although not all Christian organizations demonstrate such an aggressive stance, it certainly makes Japanese people cautious about Christianity because of its strangeness.

Only by realizing how irrational one's life is can a solution be found through revealed religion. In other words, unless one becomes aware of the impermanence of life and its related anxieties, revealed religion does not make much sense. Such awareness can be interpreted as one's incapacity for maintaining ordinary life activities. Thus the majority of Japanese dislike revealed religion, not because they are uncomfortable with the teachings themselves, but because they lack the courage to find true meaning in life through such religions. After experiencing enough sadness, pain, or depression, most people do not want to have their feelings stirred up any more, even though religion seems to delve into the meaning of life at a much deeper level. In this sense, being non-religious is an expression of self-protection against dealing with one's true self. Natural religion does not require the question "Who am I?" which often needs to be addressed. In addition, donations and other obligations are not required to participate in many rituals. Through participation in annual activities, many people find comfort when ancestral spirits and kami are worshiped.

At the same time, revealed religion itself creates its own reasons for making people stay away. For instance, reading the Bible, singing psalms and hymns, and praying may make a regular church member feel welcome, but not for those who just walk into a church service or belong to a different faith. During my ethnological field studies, I was often invited to join local Shinto festivals. While eating food and drinking rice wine (*sake*) which had been offered to the tutelary deity of the community, I felt uncomfortable worshiping their deity because I was not a parishioner of the community (*ujiko*). Foreigners living in Japan may have the same feeling when the Japanese national anthem, *kimigayo*, which literally means "His Majesty's Reign," is sung in their presence.[2] In these respects, therefore, the history of both revealed and natural religions shows obvious reasons for making the majority of Japanese people non-religious.

Notes

1. See *Nihonjin no shūkyō ishiki* surveyed by NHK in 1984, *Shūkyōshin to nihonjin* in Asahi Shinbun on May 5, 1981, and *Nihonjin no shūkyō ishiki chōsa to kōdō* in *Kokuminsei chōsa* by Monbushō surveyed every five years since 1953.

2. "Kimigayo":
Thousands of years of happy reign[s] be thine;
Rule on, my lord, till what are pebbles now
By age united to mighty rocks shall grow
Whose venerable sides the moss doth line.
(Translated by Basil H. Chamberlain)
The poem is from the tenth-century anthology *Kokinshū*, whose author is unknown. See "National Anthem." *Japan: An Illustrated Encyclopedia.* Tokyo: Kōdansha, 1993. [Translator's note]

Chapter 2

The History of Being Non-Religious

1. Kami and Buddha Live Together

In this chapter, I offer a historical analysis of how the Japanese lost their interest in Buddhist teachings. In the medieval period, between the late twelfth and fourteenth century, many people believed in the simultaneous existence of three categories: 1) kami, native deities, and buddhas; 2) the six realms, namely hell, hungry ghosts, animals, fighting warriors, humans, and heavenly beings; and 3) rebirth free from suffering.

Shinran (1173-1262), the founder of Jōdoshinshū or Shin Buddhism (the largest denominations of which today are Higashi and Nishi Honganji), was anxious about the possibility of falling into hell.[1] Although he pursued Buddhist meditation for twenty years on Mt. Hiei (near Kyoto), the center of Buddhist study at that time, Shinran could not free himself spiritually. After years of struggle, he finally attained liberation upon meeting Hōnen (1133-1212), who was sharing the Nembutsu teaching with ordinary people. According to Hōnen, anybody could attain birth in the Pure Land and become a buddha just by uttering the Name of Amida Buddha (Namu-Amida-Butsu, otherwise known as the Nembutsu). What Hōnen taught was revolutionary in Buddhist history, because he rejected any practices other than the Nembutsu.[2] At that time, becoming a monk meant seeking the way to transcend *samsāra* (i.e., this world, where people must endure various afflictions) by pursuing ascetic practices and attaining transcendental wisdom (Skt. *prajñā*). Nevertheless, both

Hōnen and Shinran realized their own limitations as well as the deeply-rooted forces within themselves, their "blind passions" (bonnō).[3]

After realizing his inability to remove these blind passions, Shinran saw that ascetic practices were of no use to him, so he started searching for an authentic Buddhist life. He decided to visit Rokkakudō (a temple located in the capital of Kyoto and which Prince Shōtoku [574-622] had built to enshrine the Bodhisattva of Compassion [Kannon]) for a hundred-day retreat, but at dawn on the ninety-fifth day, Shinran received a vision from the Prince. (In the medieval period, the custom of visiting shrines or temples to receive revelations from a kami or buddha was quite widespread). After this event, Shinran decided to visit Hōnen.

Kumagai Jirō Naozane, a well-known warrior, also took refuge in the Nembutsu teaching. In the Battle of Ichinotani between the Minamoto and Taira families, Kumagai had killed a warrior (Taira no Atsumori) who was as young as his own son, so he was haunted by a deep sense of remorse. It was Kumagai's realization of his own karma and fear of falling into hell that motivated him to visit Hōnen. Many other warriors like Kumagai also joined Hōnen's group at that time. When authorities investigated their reason for leaving duty, Hōnen advised these warriors tell them that they were simply looking for peace in the afterlife.

The joy of spiritual liberation that the ordinary people experienced was often recorded in such popular medieval tales as Konjaku monogatari and Shasekishū. For instance, one day, after a marauder listened to Hōnen explaining how even those who had committed murder could attain birth in the Pure Land through the Nembutsu, the marauder immediately shaved his head and began a journey to the west, where Amida Buddha was believed to be.

Although the wish for spiritual freedom made medieval people enthusiastic about the Buddhist teachings, and in particular Hōnen's Nembutsu, their religious feelings gradually waned soon after that. What was the reason for this?

2. The Arrival of Confucianism

Many people still sought spiritual liberation at the beginning of the Muromachi period (1333-1568), after the military regime of the Kamakura shogunate (1192-1333) had collapsed. Ashikaga Takauji (1305-1358), the first shogun of the Muromachi government, wrote a letter to Kiyomizudera, a temple in Kyoto, after he defeated his enemies Nitta Yoshisada (1301-1338) and Kusunoki Masashige (1294-1336) in the Battle of Minatogawa, an event that should have been the greatest moment of his life.

> Living in this world is just like dreaming. I need a mind of aspiration, *bodaishin*, for enlightenment. Please lead my next life into peace. Instead of enjoying the result of good karma I have accumulated in the past, please assure peace in my next life. I wish I could have pursued a monastic life. . . .[4]

Soon after this letter was written, the people's concern about the afterlife was replaced by an optimistic view of daily life. According to studies of the mottoes taught in warrior families, Confucianism prevailed in society around this time. Initially, it taught the five principles of benevolence, righteousness, decorum, judgment of good and bad, and trust (*jin gi rei chi shin*) as supplemental teachings to Buddhism and Shinto. At the same time, it was thought that various deities advocated the Confucian teachings; many people believed that various kami and buddhas would take care of them after death if such teachings were followed, even if they did not actually have faith in kami and buddhas. In other words, prayers to kami and buddhas were made only when people thought about the afterlife; observing the ethics of Confucian teachings was good enough for daily life. Thus, the search for spiritual liberation gradually ceased to exist. In the meantime, as the economy became more stable, many people started seeking ideal relationships among themselves, such as between lord and warrior, master and servant, husband and wife, parent and child, and so on.

Confucianism originally came from China, where its practitioners were mainly elite political philosophers (*shitaifu*) interested in how to achieve a harmonious society. Morality and ethics were their top priority. As Confucianism spread in Japan to warriors, wealthy merchants, and village headmen, life and death were gradually separated from each other and interest in the teachings of particular Buddhist schools waned. A growing consciousness in the seventeenth century of the "floating world" further promoted the decline of religiosity.

3. From the "World of Suffering" (*ukiyo* 憂き世) to the "Floating World" (*ukiyo* 浮き世)

The usage of the term "impermanence" (*mujō*) in ancient poems has been carefully studied. Although it is not found in the *Kojiki* or *Nihonshoki*, it appears in the *Manyōshū* compiled sometime between the fifth and eighth century. According to Mori Ryūkichi, "impermanence" and similar terms are seen among 1.4% of poems complied in the *Manyōshū*. The usage increased to 23.17% in the *Kokinshū* and to 33.14% in the *Shin kokinshū* compiled in the tenth to thirteenth centuries. The concept of impermanence prevailed by that time, particularly in Kyoto and western Japan.

Buddhism teaches that everything changes constantly (*shogyō mujō*), and that this is the cause of suffering. For instance, loved one eventually dies, wealth vanishes, and property may be destroyed in a blink of an eye by war or natural disaster. Since both material things and life are ephemeral, the recognition of impermanence makes the world one of suffering and lament (*ukiyo*).

The concept of *mujō* originally came from China, but the Japanese replaced it with the concept of *ukiyo*. The former, meaning "unproductive," was also pronounced *hakanai* (*haka* means "a section of a paddy field" or "space between fields," and *nai* means "cannot obtain"). So even today, many people say *hakaga yuku* or *hakadoru* in order to measure their productiveness in work. According to Karaki Junzō, it also meant being marginal in society. For instance, women from noble families and men excluded from politics were said to be more prone to a life of impermanence.

There were two ways to overcome this: either by 1) becoming a Buddhist through pursuing ascetic practices or taking refuge in Amida Buddha; or 2) simply by ignoring the life of impermanence, which often led one to seek enjoyment in the beauty of nature or love. Although the matter of the afterlife was still a concern for many people, it was said that Amida Buddha would welcome to his Pure Land whoever uttered the Nembutsu, so there was no reason for one to remain pessimistic. Therefore, the world of suffering (*ukiyo*) was transformed to another *ukiyo*, the "floating world," where people could just play as it were and enjoy life. The *Kanginshū* express the idea that life is too short to think about death; pleasure-seeking grew stronger during the sixteenth and seventeenth centuries, when the development of the paddy fields assured people a stable economy that allowed them to pursue leisure activities.

4. Religious Feeling in the Floating World

Ihara Saikaku (1642-1693) detailed how to enjoy life in this kind of world. According to him, one needed to make a life plan in advance, and to use numbers as a timeline for achievement. In *Nihon eitaigura* (The Japanese Family Storehouse), he explains that a person must first learn the family business from his parents starting at the age of thirteen through the next ten to fifteen years. Up to the age of forty-five, one must work hard to save money for retirement. After that, however, one may start enjoying a life of pleasure, which Ihara saw as the ultimate goal. It was also important for a person to be healthy and trusted and to pray to various deities. Ihara's idea was so influential that rich merchants of Hakata (in present-day Fukuoka prefecture) and Kawachi (present-day Osaka prefecture) advised their children to work hard and not concern themselves with the afterlife.

For Ihara, only numbers could be trusted. According to Matsuda Osamu, Ihara composed 4,000 poems the night his wife died, which means one poem every thirty-six seconds! On another occasion, he composed 23,500 poems in one day, which earned him the title "the old man of twenty thousand verses" (*nimanou*). In this way, Ihara promoted the quantity of his work so that other people could see how great he was. In his famous novel *Kōshoku ichidai otoko* (The Life of an Amorous Man), the protagonist left 3,742 women and 725 men in his life. Sexuality was also measured in quantity! Since *ichidai* means "one generation," Ihara evidently did not care about the prosperity of his children or grandchildren.

During the Tokugawa period (1603-1868), the concept of time changed greatly. Previously, a day had been divided into twelve two-hour periods; now, each period was divided into three segments of forty minutes each, which were further divided into four ten-minute periods. The ten-minute period, then, became the smallest unit by which to measure time, compared to two hours in the past. As a result, tasks were assigned to smaller periods and people became busier.

Today, the Japanese measure the value of all things in numbers, and this trend can be traced back to the Tokugawa period. Unless measured, things would lose their importance; this was the beginning of rationality. In the earlier medieval period, many people were afraid of falling into hell, as they believed in the physical existence of the six realms (as mentioned earlier). In the Tokugawa period, however, many found it impossible to believe in gods or buddhas they could not see; many sarcastic stories and jokes about hell were told at this time. For instance, in *Jigoku hakkei mōja no tawamure* (The Eight Scenes in Hell Where the Dead Play), hell is described as a place for sightseeing.

In order to be sent to heaven, it was believed that the dead needed to deceive or bribe the king of hell (*enma*), who would ultimately decide their fate. In like manner, *Sesshū gappo tsuji* (The Story Told by the Buddhist Monk *Gappō*) tells us that since the Nembutsu was inadequate for achieving birth in the Pure Land, bribery was highly recommended. Yet, those reborn in hell could still enjoy themselves by drinking *sake*, eating grilled fish, or riding in a boat when crossing the river between this and the other world.

In the medieval period, suffering was seen as the result of bad karma carried over from a past life. The conception of time changed in the Tokugawa period, so that the past and future were disconnected from the present. The present life was the center of people's concern; "clouds floating away in the sky" became a metaphor for the idea of enjoying life while one is living. The most important question, "Who am I?" lost its significance because it was not easily answered. Since the past life as well as heaven and hell were never visible, many people became uninterested in the Buddhist teachings. This kind of life perspective, similar to the life of a drifter living moment by moment, might appear unethical to those following revealed religion. However, it did not mean that people in the Tokugawa period completely denied religion. Since a sense of impermanence still remained, there was the possibility for people during this period to become religious, as the popularity of Ryōkan (1758-1831), a Sōtō Zen monk, and Matsuo Bashō (1644-1694), a poet, suggested.

In the religious climate of today, Buddhist monks like Ippen (1239-1289) and Ryōkan and poets such as Matsuo Bashō and Taneda Santōka (1882-1940) have again become popular. Ippen, the founder of Jishū, another Pure Land denomination, is known as "the wayfaring saint" or "the saint of abandonment."[5] Ryōkan took a long series of journeys in western Japan in order to share the Buddhist teachings with others. Bashō and Santōka were also travelers. All four were wanderers who ignored strict monastic codes and never discussed complex philosophies with the people. The lifestyle of these wanderers can be attractive to those living in the world of suffering and wishing to find joy in the floating world.

5. Funeral Buddhism

The concept of the floating world did not free people from anxieties concerning the afterlife. There emerged what has been termed Funeral Buddhism. Considered a rightful form of Buddhism, Funeral Buddhism remains widely practiced today in Japan. First, let us consider its system. A Buddhist priest in charge of a local temple bestows a Buddhist name (*kaimyō* or *hōmyō*) on the deceased, even though this is traditionally done for individuals while alive in order for them to be identified as a Buddhist. A *kaimyō* was originally bestowed upon those people who observed precepts, a practice still prevalent in many Buddhist organizations today (except for Shin Buddhism, which uses the term *hōmyō* [Dharma name]). The first memorial service is observed on the seventh day after death, and services are held in seven-day cycles up to the 49th day. This period is the so-called *chūin* or *chūu*, when it is said that one's next birth is not yet determined, a belief originating from India. This period is then followed by the 100th day and the first- and third-year memorial services, which come from Chinese tradition. In Japan, seventh, 13th, 17th, 25th, and 33rd year memorial services traditionally are held, and Shin Buddhists often commemorate the 50th and 100th year as well. On each occasion, all family members are obliged to gather while a Buddhist priest chants sutras in front of an altar, where there is a mortuary tablet of the deceased along with a Buddhist statue or image. In addition, family members gather at the time of *higan* and *obon* to visit the grave, where the priest often chants sutras again. Since the priest has a list of temple members, he sends the family a notice of expected memorial services as a reminder.

Comforted by Funeral Buddhism, many people have become much less interested in the original Buddhist teachings and have ceased worrying about the afterlife.

6. The Widespread Practice of Funeral Buddhism

Śākyamuni Buddha did not urge his disciples to perform a funeral for him and instead encouraged them to continue their practices. In India, until the late seventh century, it seems that a Buddhist funeral was simply chanting sutras at the scene of cremation. It was the Chinese who greatly valued funeral and memorial services because of their Confucian teaching of filial piety, in which children were required to remain faithful to their parents even after death. By accumulating merit, one is believed to have a better afterlife, so a child needed to practice good deeds for his parents, and hosting such services was viewed as the most honorable way of obtaining the merit.

At the Ryūmon Caves (*Ryūmon sekkutsu*) in China, whose construction began in the fifth century, many Buddhist statues and prayer petitions have been found, proving that many Chinese prayed for a better afterlife for the deceased. By the eleventh century, the 49th and 100th day memorial services became prevalent along with the first- and third-year ones. Copying sutras, making Buddhist statues, and building *stūpa* were also widely practiced as a means to accumulate merit.

When Buddhism came to Japan it brought these Chinese customs, and wealthy families (*uji*) adopted the rituals to comfort the spirits of the deceased, which supposedly protected their living relatives. According to Aruga Kizaemon, these families had both mythical and actual ancestors. Mystical ancestors were deities that they exclusively worshipped, and actual ones were their genealogical ancestors. For instance, the earliest ancestor of the Imperial family is *Amaterasu Ōmikami* (Great Divinity Illuminating Heaven, or Sun Goddess), ruler of the world, who is enshrined in a sacred place. At the same time, Emperor Jinmu is said to be the first ruler, even though it is not certain whether he was actually a historical figure or not. Physical ancestors were simply buried after their death, and since the Japanese did not know how to comfort their spirits, they eagerly adopted Buddhist rituals.

It is not clear why the Japanese shunned death during this time. For instance, in the Heian period (794–1185), nobles avoided physical contact with dead bodies, even loved ones. Perhaps it had something to do with the defilement of the body, as Takatori Masao suggests. Since the Emperor was believed to be sacred and immortal, the Imperial Household and those serving under him detested death. The spirit of the deceased would be elevated to the status of a kami only if the defilement were removed.

As mentioned earlier, there were no rituals in ancient times to pacify such a spirit and purify the defilement of death. If a person died from disease or misfortune, his spirit was believed to remain vengeful and threaten the lives of the living; therefore, many people were desperate for rituals to appease the spirit. Evidence of the lack of such rituals can also be found in early documents, in which it is revealed that many Japanese welcomed shamans (*zenshi* or *jukinshi*) from the Korean kingdom of Kudara (Paekche, 350-663). Thus, today's valuation of the rituals of Funeral Buddhism can be traced back to these ancient times.

Surprisingly, the Nembutsu taught by Hōnen and Shinran was later confused with the practices of this style of Buddhism, even though it was neither performed to fulfill one's egotistical desires nor to receive protection. For them, death meant instant birth in the Pure Land. However, as many people expected Amida Buddha to take care of the deceased, one's determination to become a Nembutsu follower in his present life was gradually ignored.

7. The Buddhist Concept of *Ie*

By the seventeenth century, Funeral Buddhism was practiced throughout Japan (except in Hokkaidō and Okinawa). The booming economy enabled people to hire Buddhist priests, *yamabushi* (ascetics living in remote mountain areas and said to possess magical powers), shamans, or Shinto priests as professional funeral officiators. (Shinto priests were the last to enter this occupation.) Yet in poor communities, the locals continued to have mutual help organizations for funerals (*sōshikikō*) that were in operation as late as the 1960s, when Japan achieved remarkable economic growth. Today, local communities' funeral responsibilities have been taken over mostly by Buddhist priests. (Although Shinto priest once conducted funerals for a short period, his participation in funerals was banned under the regulation of the Meiji government.)

The formation of the *ie* system, which is often mistaken for *kazoku*, meaning family, also supported Funeral Buddhism and was formed between the fourteenth and sixteenth century. *Ie* was a family unit measuring one's own production and social activities, which were central to people's lives. Yanagita Kunio, who tried extremely hard to define the identity of the Japanese people, suggests that many people desired to be enshrined by their children and descendants after death because their spirits would be worshiped and the *ie* system would thus be sustained.[6]

Funeral Buddhism became more widespread when the Tokugawa shogunate enforced the family register system at local temples (*terauke danka*), similar to the family household register system found at civic centers today. The priest officiated at funeral and memorial services, while the family was responsible for the maintenance of the temple. This system became effective at the time the shogunate tightened its policy to exclude Christians. Nearly all families were forced to affiliate with local temples in order to prove their rejection of Christianity. In return, local temples issued documents such as marriage certificates and travel permits; as a result, the temples grew more authoritative as did the priests. The shogunate took advantage of the established Buddhist organizations to monitor Christians, while the family register system supported the *ie* system in which even the lowest classes began practicing ancestral worship through Buddhist rituals.

Owing to Funeral Buddhism, the deceased were believed to become *hotoke* (see section 9) even though such notions were absent from original Buddhist teachings. As mentioned earlier, this was widely practiced by the late seventeenth century, and it is only correct to say that this kind of Buddhism led many people to turn away from the question of afterlife.

8. The Buddhist Suppression

In the Tokugawa period, Confucians became critical of Buddhists even while they did not reject Funeral Buddhism, as it was similar to Confucianism in its emphasis on filial piety and respect for ancestors. The Confucian criticism was thus self-contradictory. I mention this because the role of Confucians in this period is key in understanding today's non-religious climate among Japanese intellectuals.

In the Tokugawa period, being intellectual meant being a Confucian, one who was interested in how to achieve a harmonious society. In order to be a good Confucian, one had to avoid other religions; Buddhism was thus never accepted. At that time, Neo-Confucianism (*shushigaku*) was recognized by Japan as the official study, and a movement known as the "Theory to destroy the Buddha" (*haibutsuron*) was formed, supported by two outstanding philosophers. The shogunate employed Fujiwara Seika (1561-1619) and Hayashi Razan (1583-1657), who regarded the Buddhist teachings as meaningless and hopeless. Other Confucians such as Itō Jinsai (1627-1705), Yamazaki Ansai (1618-1682), and Ogyū Sorai (1666-1728) shared the same perception, as did scholars of Japanese classical literature and ancient writings (*kokugakusha*). There were two reasons for these attacks on Buddhism: the extravagant lives of its priests who became prosperous through Funeral Buddhism, and the increasing independence of the Confucian teachings. Ironically, these Confucians practiced Zen in the beginning, as Confucianism had been first brought to Japan by Zen (Ch'an) monks. Nevertheless, the Confucians found that the Buddhist emphasis on ascetic practice was in opposition to their interest in politics and morality. Thus, Fujiwara strove to remove Zen influence from Confucianism, which raised the initial criticism of Buddhism. For the Confucians, Zen was too self-absorbed in seeking enlightenment for oneself by isolating one from society as if indifferent to the rest of the world.

Zen monks themselves should have been more active in society, as Zen practitioners were often encouraged to return to society after experiencing self-realization in order to guide others toward it. In Mahāyāna Buddhism, bodhisattvas are said to exercise compassion in society so that Buddhist wisdom can be shared and attained. Unfortunately, the Confucians never learned this from Buddhism, and instead criticized monks for escaping from their duties and wasting food (*gokutsubushi*) without contributing to society.

The Confucians did not have much concern for the afterlife either, as they did not believe in rebirth; the Buddhist belief in transcending the realm of birth and death seemed nonsensical to them. For instance, Kumazawa Banzan (1619-1691) saw the ideas of hell and the Pure Land as primitive and uncivilized, but he was still buried at Keienji, a Buddhist temple, after a Confucian-style funeral. Hayashi arranged a Buddhist funeral for his mother-in-law and a Buddhist memorial service for his own father, as both had been Buddhists. Hayashi's wife also requested that their son's seventh year memorial service be conducted following Buddhist style. These practices made Hayashi uncomfortable, but he justified them by saying a respectable man should follow the customs of the ordinary people.

To sum up, the Confucians never resolved their fear of death, but instead searched for a productive way of living. It was up to Funeral Buddhism to comfort people through memorial services and the enshrining of ancestral spirits.

9. The Dead Become *Hotoke*

In Funeral Buddhism, the spirits of the deceased were believed to become *hotoke*. The Chinese used the character 仏 for Buddha, which the Japanese pronounce either *butsu* or *hotoke*. *Butsu*, the way Japanese refer to Buddha, has something to do with the Chinese pronunciation, while *hotoke* is very Japanese. According to *Iwanami kogo jiten* (The Dictionary of the Japanese Archaic Words Published by Iwanami), the Japanese tried to copy the Chinese sound and pronounced it *hoto*. Since *ke* means figure, *hotoke* means a figure of the Buddha, though this theory has yet to be confirmed. According to Yanagita, *hotoke* means "an enshrined spirit," in front of which an offering of food was placed in a container called *hotoki*. By the medieval period, many people came to worship this spirit at the time of *obon*. Nevertheless, Aruga Kizaemon objected to Yanagita's analysis and suggested that since the word *hotoke* was found in *Nihonshoki*, which was compiled in the early eighth century, it was already widely used in society. According to Aruga, *hotoke* came from the word *futoki*, meaning "the branch used in the ceremony to worship ancestors to bring their spirits back," and that when Buddhist rituals were adopted, the name continued to be used. Either way, it is fair to say that *hotoke* means the deceased and implies a figure of a deity, which is deeply rooted in the tradition of natural religion.

During the Tokugawa period, many people knew what *hotoke* meant. After receiving a posthumous Buddhist name and after one's funeral was performed, it was believed that a deceased person was transformed into a deity. In addition, many people started calling the dead *hotoke* which is still heard in horror movies or TV detective stories in Japan nowadays. The religious feelings once found in this word have now completely disappeared.

As long as Buddhist funeral and memorial services were properly held, anyone could become a *hotoke* after death; in this way, it was unnecessary for people to seek spiritual peace through revealed religion.

10. Religious Feeling in Natural Religion

Buddhism teaches the realization of suffering and true self, and the Buddhist practitioner tries to control the ego through various kinds of training. But how is this teaching related to Funeral Buddhism? Is it really Buddhism? Funeral Buddhism eased the fear of death, though at the same time losing sight of Śākyamuni's true message. Today, many Buddhist priests are asked to chant sutras in order to direct merit toward the deceased; likewise, many people want a posthumous Buddhist name, because they think that it assures their transformation into a *hotoke*. In other words, the better the posthumous name, the faster the spirit is transformed. Thus, the essence of the Buddhist teachings has been completely ignored.

Funeral Buddhism was a product of mixing organized Buddhist teachings with natural religion. More specifically, the latter took advantage of Buddhism, as it lacked rituals for the pacification of the dead. Some people may argue that the way the Japanese interpreted Buddhism was incorrect, or even say that Funeral Buddhism is a failure because there is no aspiration for self-realization or search for true Buddhist wisdom. At the same time, others may defend this kind of Buddhism by saying that it provides peace of mind to those afraid of death.

It is fair to say that the rejection of revealed religion, especially organized Buddhist teachings, is deeply rooted in the origin of natural religion. Many people are non-religious not because they have faith in the development of technology and a booming economy, nor because they believe in rationalization and materialism, but rather in the tradition of ancestral worship, which incorporated Buddhist rituals in order to supplement natural religion. Confucianism also helped to form today's non-religious climate. In the following chapter, I shall examine the history of the modern (Meiji) period in which organized religion was deliberately controlled, while several counter-movements to restore spirituality will also be discussed.

Notes

1. Higashi (East) and Nishi (West) Honganji: Although Honganji was officially recognized as a temple during the time of the third abbot, Kakunyo (1270-1351), Rennyo (1415-1499), the eighth abbot, developed it into a very powerful organization. Honganji was suppressed several times because its teaching gave awareness of the equality of life to its followers, which was seen as a threat to the government. However, it grew powerful enough to compete with military lords during the Warring States period (1467-1568) and tried to preserve its religious autonomy. For instance, Honganji confronted Oda Nobunaga, which resulted in the deaths of thousands of its followers. Toyotomi Hideyoshi, who eventually unified Japan, treated Honganji differently by avoiding further confrontation. After Kennyo, the eleventh abbot, passed away, Honganji was divided into two groups, supporting either Junnyo, Kennyo's third son, or Kyōnyo, his eldest. Hideyoshi appointed Junnyo to be the successor. However, when Hideyoshi died, Tokugawa Ieyasu granted Kyōnyo an estate nearby, after which Junnyo's group was known as Nishi Honganji while Kyōnyo's group was known as Higashi Honganji. [Translator's note]

2. Hōnen is known as the founder of Jōdoshū. He was born into a samurai family but was ordained at the age of fifteen, after his father was killed by his enemies. Although he was a prominent monk on Mt. Hiei, Hōnen searched for a way for ordinary people to transcend the realm of birth and death, which he eventually found in the Nembutsu teaching. In the Larger Sutra (Skt. *Sukhāvatīvyūha Sūtra*), Dharmākara Bodhisattva made forty-eight vows and upon their fulfillment became Amida Buddha. Realizing the importance of the eighteenth vow, Hōnen called it the Primal Vow, through which spiritual liberation for all could be attained. ("May I not gain possession of perfect awakening if, once I have attained buddhahood, any among the throng of living beings in the ten regions of the universe should single-mindedly desire to be reborn in my land with joy, with confidence, and gladness, and if they should bring to mind this aspiration for even ten moments of thought and yet not gain rebirth there. This excludes only those who have committed the five heinous sins and those who have reviled the True Dharma.") Gómez, Luis O, ed. and trans., *The Land of Bliss: The Paradise of the Buddha of Measureless Light: Sanskrit and Chinese Versions of the*

Sukhāvatīvyūha Sutras. Honolulu: University of Hawai'i Press and Kyoto: Higashi Honganji Shinshū Ōtani-ha, 1996, p.167. [Translator's note]

3. "Blind passions" (*bonnō*) is a comprehensive term describing all the forces, either conscious or unconscious, which make human beings think, feel, act, and speak and in which happiness, sadness, uneasiness, frustration, and pain arise. One is also attached to oneself because of this. To some extent, the human condition itself is, in fact, blind passions. Hirota, Dennis, ed. and trans. et al, *The Collected Works of Shinran,* vol. 2. Kyoto: Jōdo Shinshū Hongwanji-ha, 1997, p.172. [Translator's note]

4. Takayanagi, Kōju. *Ashikaga Takauji.* Tokyo: Shunjūsha, 1995, p.208.

5. Ippen taught that the Name of Amida Buddha accommodated both his enlightenment and the liberation of people. By distributing paper talismans on which the six letters of Namu-Amida-Butsu were written, and by chanting the Nembutsu while dancing, he acquired many followers. See "Ji sect." *Japan: An Illustrated Encyclopedia.* The major difference between Ippen and Hōnen/Shinran is that Ippen combined the Pure Land teaching with indigenous beliefs whereas Hōnen/Shinran did not. [Translator's note]

6. Yanagita Kunio's understanding of *ie* seems to be rather emotional, even though he usually analyzes ideas and events in detail. His point is that the *ie* system was carried over to the modern period.

Chapter 3

Poor Religious Understanding

1. Modernization Based on Myths

From the Meiji Restoration in 1868 to the end of World War II, the government that restored the Emperor to power manipulated both revealed and natural religions. Religious institutions, education, and businesses were also regulated. For instance, for nearly the last hundred years the Ministry of Education has greatly managed the educational system. Deregulation of various industries and markets has been slow, a concern that foreign countries often express to Japan today. In this way, Japan still continues under the bureaucracy that was first formed in the Meiji period. So what does modernization mean to Japan? Why did the Meiji government impose so many regulations? The answer is to establish a strong, centralized nation-state.

Japan sought to overcome the long-lasting feudalism that was presented under the Tokugawa shogunate. After the French Revolution, the concept of a nation-state became widespread among European countries, allowing for expansion of their empires abroad. After being forced to give up its political seclusion, Japan needed to compete with these European nations in order to receive equal treatment from them, though it was uncertain whether the Japanese people themselves wanted their country to change radically. The Meiji government freed its people from the four-class social system consisting of warriors-peasants-artisans-merchants; because of this new system, many people were able to become citizens. At the same time, however, they were obliged to pay taxes and join the military. Finally, according to the Constitution of the Empire of Japan enacted in 1889, citizens became subjects of the Emperor, while only certain groups had the right to vote.

The government was challenged by two tasks: how to characterize the nation of Japan and how to further educate the Japanese people as citizens. Although Prussia served as the model for Japan in the creation of a new political system, the Meiji government established the Emperor as its absolute monarch and promoted the ideology of the nation of Japan throughout the country. During the Tokugawa period, the Emperor had been seen merely as a puppet ruler; it was now necessary for him to regain respect as the absolute ruler of Japan. During the Meiji period, the Emperor was hailed as the descendant of *Amaterasu Ōmikami*, the Sun Goddess, whose story of the creation of Japan could be found in such early writings as *Kojiki* and *Nihonshoki.*

Modern nations can be defined as those countries having scientific technology and empirical philosophy. Each modern nation was founded on a certain ideology: For example, the founding spirit of France was liberty, equality, and brotherhood; and that of the Soviet was the proletariat movement. In retrospect, these ideologies show a form of utopianism. For Prussia, which served as Japan's model, the founding spirit was to revitalize the nation-state as modeled by ancient Greece. Although some of the ideologies of nation-states were not always rational, the nation of Japan was founded merely on a myth in which the Emperor was the central divine figure. Therefore, the government had to make tremendous efforts toward creating the Emperor system, and religion became a political tool to bolster the empire. The myth of Japan was never challenged by scientific rationalism. This was characteristic of Japan's modern religious history.

2. The Meaning of the Newly-Created "Religion" (*shūkyō*)

Today, the Japanese word *shūkyō* is translated as "religion," though it was originally a Buddhist term indicating the teaching of a specific Buddhist school. However, the Meiji government needed something that would convey a broader message.

Europe and America not only opened up Japan to westernization but also reintroduced Christianity. If Japan had simply rejected this religion, it might have been colonized and considered a "barbarian" country; with this in mind, Japanese politicians sought to defend the country without actually tolerating Christianity completely. The government lifted its ban on Christianity in the presence of Western nations, though continuing to regulate it through other means such as encouraging people to shun Christianity as a matter of course. It is striking that the exclusion of Christianity was the only policy that the Meiji government had continued from the previous regime, as Christianity grew as a threat to divinity of the Emperor.

As pressure from Western nations grew stronger, the Meiji government needed more concrete policies to deal with Christianity. By classifying this religion in the same category as Buddhism and Shinto, politicians thought that their control over it would be less conspicuous. For this reason, the new word *shūkyō* was coined around 1874. According to Aihara Ichirōsuke, it was translated from "die Religion" in German.

What is interesting, though, is that natural religion was excluded from this new classification. Since the usage of *shūkyō* only covered the aforementioned three religions, the opposite expression *mushūkyō* (no religion), indicates the lack of religion. Politicians, bureaucrats, and intellectuals during the Meiji period were blamed for dismissing natural religion as irrelevant in the context of modernization. However, if these leaders had been more confident of their own tradition and had nurtured natural religion, the implication of *shūkyō* would have been very different. The idea that natural religion formed the undercurrent of Japanese religious consciousness was forgotten, and very few scholars paid attention to it, except for Yanagita Kunio and Orikuchi Shinobu (1887-1953), two scholars of Japanese folklore whom I will discuss at greater length in Chapter 4.

Through the study of local belief systems and extensive fieldwork and linguistic research, both scholars appraised natural religion as a category of *shūkyō*. I propose that Yanagita and Orikuchi were the "theologians" of natural religion. In their investigations, although natural religion was considered folklore (*minkan shinkō* or *minkan denshō*), it still was difficult to analyze as such, since State Shinto and rapid westernization had already affected the Japanese religious mind by that time. Unfortunately, their study was often misunderstood as nationalistic as the two scholars sought to discover the uniqueness of being Japanese. Also, after World War II, as Marxism grew more influential, the study of natural religion was deemed unscientific and lacking a discussion of class. The study of natural religion has only recently started to receive the attention it deserves.

3. Revealed Religion Should Be Kept to Oneself

In thinking about the government's regulations on Christianity, we need to consider the thoughts of Inoue Kowashi (1843-1895), an advisor to the prominent statesman Itō Hirobumi (1841-1909) and who participated in the drafting of the Constitution of the Empire of Japan and the Imperial Rescript of Education. Although little attention has been paid to Inoue, I believe he was a brilliant politician, and his contribution to the founding of the nation of Japan was tremendous. Nakae Chōmin (1847-1901), a political philosopher, considered him one of the few intellectual politicians of his time.

In 1872, a year before lifting the ban on Christianity, Inoue proposed to restrict Christianity (*gekyō iken seigenan*), offering three options: to strengthen law enforcement in case of further suppression; to deregulate Christianity completely; and to educate the people to keep their beliefs to themselves. The first choice was unacceptable due to the increasing pressure from Western nations. However, it was too early to choose the second option, as it could result in uprisings among Japanese Christians themselves seeking to expand their own denominations. Inoue suggested that Japan needed to wait ten to twenty years before enacting such deregulation, even though the concept of freedom of religion had already been recognized in the West by then.

The third option was to separate religion into private and public spheres. In other words, being Christian was a matter of personal choice. The government would guarantee freedom of religion as long as Christian followers did not engage in such activities as printing the Bible, propagating the teachings, or holding Christian funerals in public, which might cause social disruption or even violate the law. This understanding of religion as a private matter to be kept to oneself was problematic but remains dominant in Japan today.

Inoue's idea was widely shared among the intellectuals at that time, including Nishi Amane, an educator and advisor to Yamagata Aritomo, one of the leading political figures of the Meiji and Taishō periods (Taishō period, 1912-1926). Although individual faith (*naishin*) was of no concern to the government, Nishi stated clearly that every citizen was obliged to obey the law, and that the government could restrict organized religious activities (*gaikei*) like building religious facilities or practicing rituals in public if they jeopardized the Emperor's system.

The idea of separating private religious faith from public life was eventually incorporated into the Constitution of the Empire of Japan, which remained in effect from November 29, 1890, to May 2, 1947. Article 28 states that "Japanese subjects shall, within limits not prejudicial to peace and order, and not antagonistic to their duties as subjects, enjoy freedom of religious belief."[1] The freedom was guaranteed conditionally as long as people remained "not prejudicial to peace and order" and "not antagonistic to their duties as subjects." According to Nakajima Sachio, the duties of a subject included paying taxes, joining the military, and refraining from adultery. At this point in time, State Shinto was not yet enforced upon the people. Later, Itō Hirobumi, presumably upon the advice of Inoue, wrote the guidelines of the Constitution in which he stated that the government would guarantee one's faith but restrict its social expression.

When members of the religious cult *Aum shinrikyō* spread sarin gas in the Tokyo subway in 1995, killing twelve people and injuring more than five thousand, many Japanese agreed that religion should remain completely private and not be expressed in public. This idea can be traced back to government policies enacted more than one hundred years ago! The 1995 tragedy was extremely appalling, but yet it also reminds me of the apathy of the Japanese people in regards to religion. In my opinion, the essence of religion, whether revealed or natural, is to share spirituality with others. If such activity is restricted, religion becomes dysfunctional.

4. The Creation of the Emperor Worship System

The leaders of Japan, now a centralized modern nation, succeeded in separating the private and public aspects of revealed religion. How, then, did the government treat natural religion (ancestor worship, local deity festivals, and the worship of higher deities)?

Modernization for Japan meant educating people in the Emperor system. As part of this education, the government distorted natural religion and discouraged the worship of ancestors and various deities. To understand how this was achieved, we must first examine the Emperor's responsibility in connection with modernization.

During the Boshin civil war (*Boshin sensō*, 1868-1869), the new leaders embraced the dignity of the Emperor and used their rallying call (*sonnō jōi*) to overthrow the Tokugawa regime. After the war, various logics were used to legitimate the Emperor's reign. On the one hand, the Emperor was confined to the palace, where he enjoyed aristocratic life without any of the rigors of being a monarch. On the other hand, Japanese commoners had been so isolated from the rest of the world during this seclusion period that they did not have any idea what a modern nation-state was. To restore his dignity, the new leaders celebrated the Emperor as the descendant of *Amaterasu Ōmikami* and urged him to publicly enshrine it so that others would follow suit and honor their own ancestral spirits, who were purportedly protected by the Sun Goddess. In this way, every citizen would come to feel indebted to the Emperor and so support the government. In short, the new leaders claimed a holy lineage for the Emperor to manipulate the ordinary people. No Emperor had previously visited Ise Shrine, where *Amaterasu Ōmikami* was enshrined, on a personal basis. In addition, the Emperor started honoring various deities by himself, as all Buddhist rituals had been removed from the Imperial Household.

Through the Ministry of Religion (*kyōbushō*) established in 1872, the government appointed Shinto and Buddhist priests to disseminate the system of Emperor worship. This was the beginning of the propagation of Shinto at a national level (*kokumin kyōka undō*). It was opposed by two groups: intellectuals voicing concern with the rise of artificial religion, and Buddhist and Shinto leaders. It appears that the Meiji leaders greatly desired to establish a state religion, partly inspired by the previous attempts of Shinto philosopher Hirata Atsutane and scholars of the Mito school at the end of the Tokugawa period. If a state religion had become the national ideology, it would have been much easier for the government to manipulate its citizens.

Nevertheless, such an attempt did not succeed. As mentioned before, pressure from England, France, and America was so strong that Japan had to lift the ban on Christianity in exchange for amending the *Ansei* Agreements, which had been signed in favor of the Western nations in 1858. With the presence of Western influence, the government was forced to give up its efforts to establish Shinto as the state religion; still, politicians continued to search for ways to promote Shinto at the state level. Shinto was noticeably excluded from religious classification, a phenomenon that I will discuss later in this chapter.

5. The Failure to Propagate Shinto

The government's attempt to establish a state religion was also opposed by bureaucrats and those holding power. Inoue Kowashi was against this proposed policy, as he had studied the history of Europe, in which various attempts to establish a state religion had resulted in violent uprisings. After visiting Europe in 1871, Inoue insisted that the government not foster Shinto formally, but rather utilize religion as a political tool for manipulating social order (*chian no gu*).

Shimaji Mokurai (1838-1911), a Nishi Honganji priest, expressed his opposition from a Buddhist perspective. This denomination had good relations with the government because the leaders of Nishi Honganji and some politicians including Itō Hirobumi and Kido Kōin, came from the same area, Chōshū domain (present-day Yamaguchi prefecture). Shimaji was sent to Europe to observe its religious climate and relationship between religion and state. While in France, he heard news of Japan's plan to propagate Shinto and immediately sent the government a proposal, entitled "Critique of the Three Principles" (*sanjō kyōsoku hihan kenpakusho*), now regarded as Japan's first appeal for religious freedom.[2] According to Shimaji, the establishment of a state religion would challenge an entity of transcendence and revealed the arrogance of man. In a so-called civilized nation, religion must be separated from politics, allowing people the freedom to choose based on their different spiritual needs. Shimaji also warned that the simultaneous propagation of Shinto and Buddhism would make people confused.

Although it is difficult to imagine today, both the Higashi and Nishi Honganji Temples financed the Meiji government tremendously. For example, Higashi Honganji donated 28,000 *ryō* (about $1.7 million today) in 1868, while the Nishi Honganji exchanged worthless bonds of 30,000 *ryō*, issued by the Grand Council of State, for hard currency.³

Around the same time that Shimaji submitted his proposal to the government, Mori Arinori, Japan's first envoy to Washington, also opposed the attempt to establish a state religion and proposed "Religious Freedom in Japan" (*nihon ni okeru shinkyō no jiyū ni tsuite*) in 1872.

Shinto priests also opposed the politicians, who confused Shinto with Buddhism, by stressing that Shinto was different from both Buddhism and Christianity. According to Japan's first religious journal (*kyōgi shinbun*), Shinto was regarded as the performance of national rituals and should not be judged by individual faith (*Shinto o motte shūkyō to nasu wa kōshitsu no kakin taru koto*).

Eventually, the establishment of a state religion was abandoned in the face of these strong oppositions, and the Ministry of Religion was dismantled. Nevertheless, by distinguishing Shinto from religion, the government continued to propagate the system of Emperor worship, and later achieved success in this project.

6. Distinguishing Shinto from Religion

If the government's attempt to make Shinto a state religion violated the Constitutional freedom of religion, it should nevertheless be distinguished from religion. The aforementioned religious journal stated that the previous error made by the Ministry of Religion was to treat Shinto as one form of religion. Shinto was redefined as the way of conducting imperial rituals, by which the Emperor enshrined *Amaterasu Ōmikami* and consoled those subjects who had sacrificed their lives for him.

For Nishi Sawanosuke, Shinto was "the public way of

heaven and earth" (*tenchi no kōdō*), "the energy of the universe" (*sekai no genki*), or simply "the energy of the nation" (*kokka no genki*), and as such, should not be regarded in the same category as Christianity and Buddhism. In addition, when the Office of Shinto Rituals (*jingikan*) was established, (*jinkan yūshi jingikan secchi chinjōsho*), Shinto leaders urged the priests of all shrines, large or small, to perform the state's rituals because Shinto was considered "the center of the state's spirit" (*kokka seishin no fu*) and "the true form of its worship" (*shinsei no jingidō*). This was distinguished from other forms of Shinto, such as "superstitious Shinto" (*kitō bokusōteki Shinto*) or "religion of Shinto" (*shūkyō shugi Shinto*). The prosperity of the state depended on the practice of the true form of the state's rituals.

Although Shinto was seen as "the Great Vehicle" (*daidō*) and superior to both Christianity and Buddhism, the government did not launch its propagation drive immediately; if it had officially done so, the result would have been merely the revival of the ancient political system, which was already rejected.

In this regard, Inoue Kowashi reasoned that Shinto was the tradition of the Imperial Household and rule of the state (*chōken*); therefore, state citizens should follow it. Inoue further stated that while a few scholars of national learning (*kokugaku*) in the end of Tokugawa period saw Shinto as a religion, they were the minority and were indeed wrong, as Shinto offered rituals to honor ancestors, which was different from making a prayer and worshipping in a religious mode (*kyōken*). In this way, the government was able to propagate Shinto without violating constituted freedom of religion or offending either Buddhists or Christians.

7. Shin Buddhist Leaders Support the Distinction Between Shinto and Religion

According to Ashizu Uzuhiko, Shin Buddhist leaders also supported the differentiation between Shinto and religion. Although Shimaji addressed the issue of freedom of religion for the first time in Japanese history, politicians such as Itō Hirobumi, Inoue Kaoru (1835-1915), and Katsu Kaishū (1823-1899), as well as the philosopher Fukuzawa Yukichi (1834-1901), had already understood this by the end of the Tokugawa regime.

Strangely enough, it is said that Shimaji learned the concept of
freedom of religion from them. What was unique in Shimaji was
that he put it into practice.

In order to understand Shimaji's stance, the Shin Buddhist
teaching of secular and spiritual rules (ōbō and *buppō* or
shinzoku nitairon) must be first understood. The former deals
with secular laws and moral values, while the latter denotes the
Buddhist Dharma, specifically the Nembutsu teaching of Hōnen
and Shinran. The entire Honganji organization began to accept
the notion of separate secular and spiritual rules during the
sixteenth century, when it grew powerful enough to repel the
domination of regional warlords in particular Oda Nobunaga
(1534-1582), who first tried to unify Japan. At the same time,
Honganji leaders had to deter their followers from escalating the
violence, and so a compromise between spiritual expression and
social rules was proposed; the followers were encouraged to keep
their faith (*shinjin*) to themselves. Since then, this dual principle
has been taken for granted by Honganji leaders, who teach their
followers to be obedient to authority. During the Tokugawa
period, the two-rule teaching was used as a political tool by
authorities, thereby preserving Shin Buddhist authority as well.

Religion often transcends worldly values; for this reason, it
differs from morality and ethics. Since Shin Buddhist followers
were expressive of their religious sentiments and embraced
notions of equality, their autonomy often clashed with the
authority of regional lords. This was the reason for Oda's deep
dislike of Honganji, and it is said that his attempts to unify the
country were delayed due to Shin Buddhist resistance. The
Nembutsu teaching was also banned later in some areas,
including the Satsuma domain (present-day Kagoshima
prefecture).

During the Meiji period, the split between secular and
religious realms was continually taken for granted in both
Higashi and Nishi Honganji Temples, while Shinto, in the form
of Emperor worship, still colored secular rules. When the
establishment of Emperor worship swept the country, Shin
Buddhist leaders had to come to terms with Shinto rituals in
order to survive. This was not easy for them; Hōnen clearly
taught that to practice the Nembutsu with a sincere mind was the
only cause for birth in the Pure Land, and the worship of various

deities and even other buddhas and bodhisattvas was therefore unnecessary. Shin Buddhists refused to decorate the inside and outside of their homes with pine sprigs (*kadomatsu*) at New Year, and rejected *obon* events welcoming ancestral spirits. Because of their unique traditions, Shin Buddhists were often considered ignorant of ordinary social practices (*monto mono shirazu*) and were persecuted by the government and other Buddhist institutions. Even today, while many Japanese families tend to have two altars at home, one Buddhist (*butsudan*, where ancestral mortuary tablets are often enshrined) and the other Shinto (*kamidana*), quite a few Shin Buddhists have only one altar containing only an image of Amida Buddha.

Returning to our discussion of the Meiji period, the leaders of both Higashi and Nishi Honganji Temples compromised with social regulations by taking advantage of the distinction between the secular and religious. In addition, in order to avoid any confrontation with the government, they urged their followers to worship Shinto deities, reasoning that this would eventually lead them to take refuge in Amida Buddha. In other words, the followers were required to become subjects of the Emperor and to accept Shinto while entrusting themselves in Amida at the same time; distinguishing Shinto rites from religion was the only way for the leaders to convince their followers.

According to Shimaji, Shinto simply provided the rituals by which to honor ancestors, so it should not be considered a religion. However, Confucianism and Buddhism provided the necessary spiritual guidance. The Office of Shinto Rituals was set up in order to organize Shinto rites, and it had nothing to do with the propagation of religion. His stance was almost identical to the views of Inoue Kowashi! Shimaji further stated that the various deities of Shinto represented those who had dedicated their lives to the country. Thus, worshiping these deities, visiting their shrines, and making donations were ways to express gratitude to them. If a person was too lazy to do this, he should be ashamed for not honoring the teachings of his ancestors.

Another Shin Buddhist priest, Nanjō Shinkō, also agreed with Shimaji. According to Nanjō, the ideology of Shinto was to connect the universe with the individual, however, as this was rather abstract and hard to implement, Confucianism and Buddhism served as the means for this connection. When the system of Emperor worship was promoted, the leaders of both Honganji organizations explained to their priests that worshiping Shinto deities was a service to the country and urged the priests not to be concerned about regarding such rituals as religion. In essence, by distinguishing Shinto from religion, Shin Buddhists could accept the system of Emperor worship and even voluntarily support it. As a result, Shin Buddhist spiritual expression was replaced by an ethical concern to support Emperor worship, although a few Shin Buddhist priests did attempt to restore spirituality to secular rules and demonstrate Buddhist compassion in society. This will be discussed in the last section of this chapter.

8. The Distortion of Natural Religion

The Japanese religious mind is often criticized for mixing various beliefs. In my opinion, this is due to the confusion that began when the government propagated the system of Emperor worship and State Shinto. This system, almost equivalent to a state religion, was important because bureaucrats needed to centralize power. The government interfered with the religious lives of ordinary people whose spiritual identity had been gradually lost so that they could not counter such an attack on tradition. Within this history, I would like to explore how natural religion changed.

Before the system of Emperor worship swept the country, many people worshiped kami and buddhas at the same time. For instance, at the entrance of most houses there was a space just inside called "the space on the soil floor" (*doma*), where the deities of water and fire were enshrined. On the doorsill, another deity was enshrined, and in the wood-floored main room, on the central sunken hearth (*irori*), either a Buddhist or Shinto altar was placed in which ancestral spirits were honored along with the local deity. Finally, in the guestroom, there was an ornate Shinto altar, in which an amulet from a prestigious shrine (such as Ise, Hachiman, Kasuga or Kashima) was often placed. It is said that a wife served the three deities first and her husband last.

Many homes built before the Meiji period took traditional building styles as their inspiration. For instance, the *doma* was presented in homes during the Yayoi period (ca. 300 BCE to ca.

300 AD). The wood-floored main room was reminiscent of *shinden zukuri*, the main Japanese architectural style of noble residences during the Heian period. The guestroom of a house followed *shoin zukuri*, the major residential architectural style of military leaders used between the middle of the fourteenth and the beginning of the seventeenth century. The ranking of these deities is significant in the structure of houses, in which the further toward the guestroom from the entrance, the more elevated was the deity enshrined. In short, this classification corresponded with the way the Japanese belief system developed—worshiping one's own ancestral spirits first, the deity in the community, and then more powerful divine beings. This common belief system was a combination of peculiarity and universality, which was also shared in community.

Prayers to kami and buddhas were quite different before the Meiji period. These involved everyday wishes that were directed to the kami, while concerns about the afterlife were directed toward buddhas. Different types of prayers served the spirituality of the people at different levels. However, this tradition altered when the government promoted the system of Emperor worship, in which there was a change in the ranking of the deities. Two policies were imposed: one closely differentiating between Buddhism and Shinto (*shinbutsu hanzenrei*) and the other categorizing all Shinto shrines throughout the country (*jinja gōshirei*). As mentioned earlier, the first policy brought about the movement to "abolish Buddha and destroy Śākyamuni," in which Buddhist influences were completely removed from Shinto shrines. After this spiritual upheaval, prayers to buddhas disappeared. Was everybody then expected to pray to kami for comfort in the afterlife?

Regarding the second policy, all Shinto shrines were classified into two categories: those belonging to the lineage of the supreme deity *Amaterasu Ōmikami,* and all the rest. When the Office of Shrine Affairs was set up, the Ise Shrine, which enshrined *Amaterasu Ōmikami,* was regarded as the highest of shrines. A Shinto priest appointed by the government became the chief administrator of local prestigious shrines and worked in service of the Emperor. Shinto priests with inherited positions were removed. As the government's budget was limited, many shrines merged so that only one was permitted in each area. As a result, some people were forced to give up their faith in the local deity and instead respect one enshrined in a neighboring village. At that time, fewer than two thousand shrines were officially recognized at the national, prefectural, and other administrative levels, even though there were about 110,000 shrines total throughout Japan. In addition, the government banned the worship of unknown deities considered superstitious, shamanic, or primitive. Local communal faith, the root of religious life, was thus lost with the implementation of Emperor worship. Yet, not many people perceived the nature of this change in their daily lives.

The style of Shinto worship was also redefined; namely, prayer was removed from rituals, and according to Inoue Kowashi, people at this time were supposed to clap their hands three times without praying. Nevertheless, wasn't it supposedly prayer itself that naturally promoted them to clap their hands and bow? It seems reasonable to think that rituals without prayer are not religious, and perhaps should not even be regarded as rituals in the normal sense of the word. The government's interpretation was disastrous for Shinto, but it was implemented to promote Emperor worship and the Shinto priests accepted it. In this way, Shinto rituals grew to be considered non-religious acts.

Yanagita recognized that many Japanese traditionally worshiped in two ways: *kigan* and *keishin*. The former meant worshipping a local deity enshrined by the community (*ujigami*, originally means the tutelary deity of an *uji* or clan. In early Japan, there were many clan families and their members; each group had its own ancestral deity to worship), while the latter was merely paying one's respect to various deities. While traveling around Japan, many people began to realize the value in showing respect to unfamiliar deities, even though personal prayers were never made in their presence. This idea was similar to the concept of freedom of religion, thus, the Japanese had already been exposed to the idea of respecting others' faiths long before the introduction of this Western concept, as found in European nations. Needless to say, the system of Emperor worship destroyed this Japanese freedom of religion.

In summary, although the attempts to establish a state religion failed, the government was successful in propagating Emperor worship by distinguishing Shinto from religion. This enabled Buddhists and Christians to feel less offended and to accept Shinto rituals into their own personal lives without problem. However, natural religion and local Shinto belief systems were distorted by Emperor worship.

9. Poor Religious Perspective

It is quite obvious that both revealed and natural religions were manipulated by the state. Faith was to be kept to oneself, and expressing spiritual concerns in society was prohibited. The government discouraged the worship of ancestors and community deities, and dealt with them by changing their classification. For instance, Izumo Shinto, which enshrines *Ōkuninushi no Mikoto*, the guardian of the region and creator of Japan, was attacked because the government had already recognized *Amaterasu Ōmikami* as the nation's creator.[4] Also, *Tenrikyō*, a new religion derived from Shinto and other native religious tradition, became part of Sect Shinto and was monitored by the government.

State Shinto was recognized as merely ritualistic and not as a religion. Intellectuals and politicians viewed natural religion to be inferior to revealed religion, due to the influence of Western culture and Christianity. With the goal of catching up with the West in modernization, the government interfered in every aspect of life. Only a few people, including religious leaders, resisted. Although the movement to "abolish Buddha and destroy Śākyamuni" had badly damaged the Buddhist community, Funeral Buddhism still remained strong as it addressed people's anxieties about the afterlife. Hence, the Japanese felt little need to search for further spirituality. To some extent, being non-religious was an excuse to not question the law of the land and the government's system. In addition, scientific development and rationalization prevailed in society, leading people to become less interested in revealed religion.

Our lives are limited, and we are unsure whence we come and what will happen to us after death; isn't it necessary, then, to find the meaning of life and gain the wisdom of self-understanding? Although such activity belongs in the hands of each individual, religion can certainly serve as a guide to enrich our lives. Unfortunately, after the Meiji period, many people abandoned this endeavor.

10. Attempts to Restore Spirituality

Kiyozawa Manshi (1863-1903) and Takagi Kenmyō (1864-1914), both priests of Higashi Honganji, attempted to restore spirituality to Shin Buddhism, although they never became central figures in their own times.

Kiyozawa was born into a low-ranking samurai family in Nagoya, but due to his extraordinary talents and under the recommendation of Higashi Honganji priests, he received a scholarship from the head temple and entered Tokyo Imperial University (present-day Tokyo University). In college Kiyozawa studied Hegelian philosophy under Ernest F. Fenollosa, and in graduate school he majored in religious philosophy. In fact, Kiyozawa was the first religious philosopher in Japan. After graduating, he moved to Kyoto in 1888 to be the principal of a Kyoto municipal middle school supported by his denomination. In spite of a promising future, Kiyozawa abandoned a comfortable life and pursued a program of asceticism in order to seek spiritual truth. He gave up smoking and drinking, refrained from eating meat, and separated himself from his family, dedicating himself to reforming the Higashi Honganji organization and restoring the Shin Buddhist teaching. In his tireless effort, however, Kiyozawa contracted tuberculosis and died at the age of forty. His life is described as the "minimum possible" (e.g., living as materially simply as one can), and he was involved in the spiritual movement (*seishin shugi*) in which spirituality was an expression of *shinjin* as found in the Shin Buddhist tradition.

Kiyozawa tried to reconstruct the Shin Buddhist teaching by using Western concepts. One of his key concepts was that of "the finite and the infinite." It is natural for human beings to long for eternity and look for a spiritual foundation, since life is finite. Such infinity is found in Amida Buddha, and if spirituality is established, life based on *shinjin* becomes our most important concern, while obedience to the Emperor or the central government is only secondary. Kiyozawa was able to examine society after he rediscovered himself in the infinite world of spirituality and after realized his own limitations. He also thought that morality or loyalty to the Emperor could never lead to spiritual attainment, due to the imperfections of all man-made regulations. Therefore, if religion confronts authority and leads people to question the political system, it is only unavoidable.

Kiyozawa passed away a year before the Russo-Japanese war (1904-1905), so his teaching never became widespread. In a sense, Takagi Kenmyō was the one who directly confronted the Emperor worship system, even though his relationship with Kiyozawa was unclear. According to Izumi Shigeki, Takagi was born into a confectionary business in Aichi prefecture and was ordained at Higashi Honganji at the age of seventeen, after which he moved to Wakayama prefecture to share the Shin Buddhist teaching with coal miners there. He eventually settled down in the Shingū area, though his reason for choosing this area is unclear. Takagi became the minister of Jōsenji, a temple located in a residential area of *burakumin*, Japan's largest minority group subject to social discrimination. At first, Takagi seemed merely sympathetic to the *burakumin*'s lives of hardship, but as he started looking into his own mind, he found prejudice there. At the same time, he understood that this prejudice was formed in certain historical situations, promoted by whoever accepted it, and supported by the government for various political reasons. Therefore, he decided to liberate himself from such discrimination and to liberate those who were discriminated against at the same time. Following this decision, Takagi opposed the Russo-Japanese War and criticized state prostitution in his district.

Takagi's determination was based on his religious convictions, in which his mind became parallel with the compassion of Amida Buddha leading everyone toward self-realization. According to the Shin Buddhist teaching, the difference between rich and poor, young and old, men and women, or moral and immoral is unimportant to the functioning of such compassion. If one awakens to one's true self and embraces compassion, how can one accept social discrimination?

Unfortunately, the Buddhist community in general did not support Takagi, because the government and the headquarters of Higashi Honganji controlled the priests and their expressed beliefs. Takagi eventually became isolated from his dissenters but found associates among the socialists and a few Christians, even though his stance was quite different from theirs. For Takagi, socialism merely provided a way to express Amida's compassion; he never intended to reform society along ideological lines. For this reason, as Izumi says, Takagi saw himself simply as the resident priest of Jōsenji.

Nevertheless, owing to his relationship with these socialists, Takagi was implicated in the High Treason Incident (*taigyaku jiken*) in 1910, a government conspiracy intended to eliminate all socialists. In this incident, twenty-five men and one woman, including Takagi and his friends from the Shingū area, were interrogated and given an unfair trial. On January 18, 1911, all of them were found guilty; Kōtoku Shūsui (1871-1911), the accused ringleader, was executed with eleven others about a week later. Takagi himself was imprisoned in Akita in northern Japan, but without any hope of amnesty, he hanged himself on June 24, 1914.

A few other Buddhist priests were also involved in this incident, proving that, true to their teachings, they did confront the government. Takagi was arrested and imprisoned because of his sincerity in embracing the Nembutsu teaching. His religious convictions did not stop him from acting in accord with this.

Although not directly taking over Kiyozawa's spiritual ground, Takagi shared Kiyozawa's same drive, apart from their affiliation with Higashi Honganji. To both men, religion was not merely a personal matter.

Unfortunately, after the High Treason Incident, religious expression died out in society and religion lost its vitality. Kiyozawa's spirituality was taken for granted as a personal matter and his followers, including Akegarasu Haya (1877-1967), urged many people to be dutiful to the Emperor and support nationalism. Further, the Higashi Honganji administration, in order to show loyalty to the government, defrocked and excommunicated Takagi on the very day his verdict was handed down; this was a symbolic, complete defeat of the spiritual realm by secular power.

It is reasonable to say that the movement to restore spirituality failed, as Ishikawa Takuboku (1886-1912) has pointed out. After the High Treason Incident, though Japan became increasingly isolated from the rest of the international community, the government had succeeded in making religion a strictly private matter. Buddha's compassion was replaced by sympathy for others, and social problems were ignored. As a result, many people lost their deep religious feelings, and it is unlikely that self-examination concerning non-religious feelings will again become prevalent in society in the near future.

As far as Higashi Honganji is concerned, it reinstated Takagi into its ministry in 1996 and publicly apologized to him after more than eighty years. Takagi's significance has recently been re-evaluated due to the gradual revival of Kiyozawa's spiritual movement. Nevertheless, Takagi's execution and the suffering of his family can never be completely redressed.[5]

Notes

1. "Constitution of the Empire of Japan." *Japan: An Illustrated Encyclopedia.*
2. The Three Principles are: 1) to respect kami and love the nation; 2) to understand the nature of heaven and the duty of the subject; and 3) to remain loyal to the Emperor and Court. See Ketelaar, James E. *Of Heretics and Martyrs in Meiji Japan.* New Jersey: Princeton University Press, 1993, p. 106. [Translator's note]
3. According to Mishima Ryōchū, the abbot of Nishi Honganji at that time planned to move the administration office from Kyoto to the front of the Imperial Palace in Tokyo, to serve the Emperor and nation. If the plan had been carried out, Nishi Honganji would have purchased one of the most expensive pieces of land in Japan, an area between Marunouchi and Hibiya near Tokyo station.
4. *Ōkuninushi no Mikoto* is a Shinto deity said to be either a son or descendant of *Susano'o no Mikoto*, the brother of *Amaterasu Ōmikami*. *Ōkuninushi no Mikoto* literally means "the Great Deity of the Land," and is said to be benevolent and valiant. See "Ōkuninushi no Mikoto" and "Susano'o no Mikoto." *Japan: An Illustrated Encyclopedia.* [Translator's note]
5. On Kiyozawa and Takagi, see Ama, Toshimaro. "Towards a Shin Buddhist Social Ethics." In *The Eastern Buddhist,* new series vol. xxxiii, 2 (2001): pp.35-54. [Translator's note]

Chapter 4

Religion and the Value of Just Being Ordinary

In this chapter, the "value of just being ordinary" (*nichijō shugi*) will be considered in relation to the Japanese religious mind. As mentioned earlier, Yanagita Kunio was a scholar in the field of natural religion; it is now necessary to consider his analyses and to show how his evaluation of just being ordinary affected his attitude toward both revealed and natural religions.

1. Washing Off One's Innate Nature

In 1937, Yanagita gave a lecture on *Heibon to hibon* (The Ordinary and Extraordinary) at the Second High School (present-day Tōhoku University in Miyagi prefecture), expressing his concern that the history of everyday people's lives in Japan had been ignored. The lecture was addressed to young people with promising futures, and Yanagita felt it necessary for such students to understand such a history. He questioned the way Japanese history was being taught, for it focused solely on the lives of heroes and the famous. This view was based on records preserved by those in positions of authority and power, whose accounts included little about lives of ordinary people. Without studying the people, how can their current problems be identified and solutions found? For instance, it has often been said that life in the Tokugawa period was miserable as people repeatedly endured peasant revolts, famine, and natural disasters. Little has been said on daily life, but in fact, local stories show that even ordinary lives were rich in all emotional aspects. According to Yanagita, it was more important and meaningful to understand the lifestyle of one's own ancestors than to study the life of Minamoto no Yoritomo (1147-1199), the first shogun of the Kamakura regime, or to learn about the significance of a battle fought between the Minamoto and Taira families.

In this lecture, Yanagita stated that as the result of modernization, Japanese education after the Meiji Restoration of 1868 discarded the traditional lifestyle as merely ordinary and thus unimportant. Nevertheless, it was still questioned whether state education would enrich the lives of ordinary people. On the one hand, he saw the problems of tradition, evident in such sayings as: "The nail that stands out gets hammered down" or "the sizes of acorns are all the same." On the other hand, Yanagita felt that the mere rejection of traditions, which sustained community life, would not create a bright future. Therefore, Yanagita insisted that the re-evaluation of traditional ways was necessary, and the wisdom of shared community life needed to be taught; unless this was done, education in Japan would continue to be self-contradictory. For instance, while forcing the majority of students to remain in the mold of the ordinary, schoolteachers occasionally encourage a few talented ones to enter prestigious elite universities, and then attribute the students' success on simply their education.

Although more than sixty years have passed since this lecture, the denigration of ordinary life and the promotion of the exceptional still remains prevalent in education. Today, it is hard to find a person who positively respects an ordinary lifestyle, and rural communities are steadily losing their values as well, as most people prefer to live in cities. However, at the same time, an inclination toward an ordinary way of life is still regarded as the best means of avoiding obvious mistakes. For instance, in order to send their child to a good university, parents have to work very hard so that their son or daughter can receive private tutoring. Public schools still regulate the talent of each student and emphasize harmony in class. Therefore, if a child wants to express his true talent, the child's parents, who are often very obedient to the organizations to which they belong, tell their child to hold back as they are concerned about bullying and special attention that he might receive from teachers.

Under these circumstances, a student becomes passive and worries constantly about the reaction of others. This is one negative aspect of the emphasis on the value of just being ordinary; unfortunately, this is still widespread within today's society and contributes to the non-religious climate nowadays, in which revealed religion is seen as extraordinary or different and discussing religion is considered pointless.

The ritual of washing off one's innate nature (*saganagashi*), which Yanagita introduced in this lecture, illustrates this point quite well. The word *saga* literally means "nature" or "appearance" and indicates innate nature, destiny before birth, good and bad things, or good and bad.[1] He describes this ritual as follows:

> The villagers seek to avoid trouble today. However, in the past they were strongly motivated by something else. On the fifteenth of January of each year, *saganagashi* and other festivals were held along the River Tenryū in Shinshū (present-day Nagano prefecture). The word *saga* literally means "good and bad," or any event causing trouble. Therefore, the villagers avoided even good things in order to maintain peace in their daily lives.[2]

Yanagita made similar remarks elsewhere and it is obvious that he was quite interested in this ritual:

> *Saga* literally means "good and bad things" – either way it was seen as a cause of trouble. In general, villagers disliked unusual events and desired peace. For this reason, on the seventh of every January, decorations used in the New Year's festivals were thrown into the river. Why, therefore, were they so superstitious?[3]

Although the dates of the rituals in these descriptions differ, the villagers believed in eliminating anything that would disturb their ordinary lives on this occasion. This kind of festival may have existed throughout Japan in the past, but I first heard of it when visiting Ōgamijima, one of the Miyakojima chain of islands in Okinawa prefecture. The festival there called *Toutaminigai,* in which local people symbolically shout curses into a container and then seal it, after which they place it in a particular spot, such as at a crossroads, where a funeral procession passes. At the same time, complimenting others is frowned upon, as it is believed that those who are not praised become jealous and start cursing them. For this reasons, magical words are chanted for protecting the local people from misfortune triggered by both good and bad languages. This festival shows the villagers' avoidance of both abusive and complimentary words, following the concept of *saganagashi.*

According to Yanagita, this mentality could be expressed by the saying, "All people must be average and ordinary." This was the power of tradition and the source of reciprocal trust promoted by their ancestors. In the minds of the villagers, even a good event benefiting oneself was detrimental to the harmony of the community.

2. Yanagita's Inclination Toward Ordinary Thinking (*jinjō shikō*)

Yanagita sought to extract the life perspective of ordinary people by analyzing their way of thinking. His extensive research reveals his sympathies to the people's spirituality. Yanagita's study also shows his personal preferences and reflects his own background, for example, in his highlighting of ancestral worship and his dislike of Shin Buddhism, which will be discussed at the end of this chapter. Yanagita himself was inclined toward the principle of just being ordinary, and this is seen in his various writings.

In his essay *Yama no jinsei* (Life in the Mountains), Yanagita showed how much he was moved by the feelings of ordinary people.

> Faith demands that life be natural. It is unnecessary for people to worship the sun, moon, and stars, because they are not within their reach. Having faith means seeking everyday happiness, through day and night and in the four seasons (*jinjō no kōfuku*). To avoid trouble that would disturb their ordinary lives, people worshiped the local deities of the mountains and wilderness or of the sea and river, by holding festivals and serving them.[4]

For Yanagita, the deities that the Japanese worshiped did

not require pantheons or gigantic temples, as they were very close to the people. Encountering the sacred was a habitual experience, so God and Buddha were unnecessary in the search for everyday happiness. The Japanese people liked their religion simple, in accordance with their ordinary lives.

The information above is found in *Nōson kazoku seido to kanshū* (The System of a Village Family and its Customs), which was written between 1927 and 1928; *Yama no jinsei* was published in 1925. Since it is unusual for Yanagita to repeat descriptions in different publications, it is fair to say that this reflects his own strong preferences.

In another essay, *San Sebasuchan* (Saint Sebastian), Yanagita describes his own religious background, including his worship of ordinary deities and his avoidance of revealed religion. He reflects upon why portraits of St. Sebastian were so popular in Europe. He references the image of a young, naked martyr bound to a tree with a rope and bleeding from arrows shot into his arms, chest, and belly. Yanagita thought that Europeans admired the selfless Sebastian, as his faith was strong enough to endure pain. This may be good propaganda for Christians, but for those quietly enjoying life, including Yanagita himself, such a state of mind was problematic. In his opinion, revealed religion should be avoided if ordinary life were to be maintained, even if that religion is held in high esteem.

Based on his personal preferences, Yanagita classified the Nembutsu into two categories: that recited for the consolation of the deceased and that taught by Hōnen. The Nembutsu was first practiced right after Buddhism was brought to Japan. In one instance, a group of monks lined up along the street to recite the Nembutsu for Emperor Daigo's (885-930) funeral procession; even after the burial ceremony, Buddhist novices gathered at the grave for further chanting. From that time onwards, the Nembutsu was performed at all aristocratic funerals. At the same time, Kūya (903-972), the initiator of the Dancing Nembutsu (*odori nembutsu*), gathered corpses abandoned in the city of Kyoto, cremated them, and held memorial services for them. He walked around the city beating a drum and reciting the Nembutsu. When Funeral Buddhism became popular, the Nembutsu was seen as a way to alleviate the spirits of the deceased. Until very recently, small groups called *nembutsukō* were occasionally formed in communities for funerals and memorial services in which the Nembutsu was chanted and religious poems were sung. Yanagita praised this because it was liberating for people who feared death and who had been taught that memorial services would console the spirits of the deceased.

It should be noted that in ancient Japan, before the introduction of Buddhism, the understanding of death was rather narrow. At that time, it was believed that the spirits of the deceased were vengeful. As mentioned in Chapter 2, Buddhism originally had nothing to do with ritualistic practices for the dead. However, under the influence of filial piety that came from China, ritual offerings to the Buddha were applied to the pacification of spirits as well, and people began to pray for a better afterlife for the deceased. Thus, the Pure Land became a place where the deceased were embraced by Amida Buddha. Although this pacification of the dead reduced Buddhism to the level of exorcism, it seemed extremely attractive in those times.

On the one hand it is fair to say that Buddhism grew popular as a means to ensure a propitious afterlife, and the chanting of the Nembutsu for the spirits of the dead contributed to the stability of ordinary life. On the other hand, Hōnen taught that the Nembutsu was for one's own liberation and that anyone who recited this would be born in the Pure Land and become enlightened. In this sense, spiritual liberation was based on one's understanding that Amida embraced one solely on one's practice of the Nembutsu. Yanagita saw this as "chanting for one's own sake" (jikayō no nembutsu) and therefore individualistic. Although the first type of the Nembutsu was to console the spirits of the dead, and it was thus ideal for community members to pray for the stability of their own ordinary lives, Hōnen taught that a person could become a buddha (not hotoke), through Amida Buddha's compassion, and there was no need for family members to perform any special practices for the dead. As a result, annual events such as obon services or New Year's celebration (during which the spirits of the dead, their families, and the community were supposedly united) could be abandoned; traditional faith was gradually lost. Yanagita's main concern was that the sole practice of the Nembutsu that Hōnen and Shinran had taught would jeopardize the bonds within the community that natural religion had gradually built.

Yanagita's analysis needs to be examined in a historical context. When Rennyo (1415-1499), the eighth abbot of Honganji, created a more powerful organization in Shin Buddhism, the Nembutsu practice became widespread, even during the period of feudal warfare in the sixteenth century. This was because the teaching was shared by communities throughout the country and because it did not promote an individualistic way of living, as Yanagita assumed. In fact, the sole practice of Nembutsu was well received, as there was a need at that time to strengthen bonds among people. For instance, the autumn harvest festival was replaced by *Hōonkō*, the most important event among Shin Buddhists which honored their founder, Shinran.

3. How Should Bad Events Be Perceived?

Despite wishing for stability, a person sometimes gets involved in unforeseen events and is victimized; it is therefore impossible to predict the future. How should unexpected events then be perceived? The answer to this can also be found in the value of just being ordinary. In his autobiography, *Kokyō shichijūnen* (Seventy Years in My Hometown), Yanagita wrote a book review of *Jūemon no saigo* (The Death of Jūemon) written by Tayama Katai (1871-1930) in 1902. Although Yanagita and Tayama had been close friends, none of Tayama's novels other than *Jūemon no saigo* interested Yanagita, as they were often based on stories he had already told the writer. Nevertheless, Yanagita praised this book even in his later years, although he never explained precisely why it moved him. The novel may be summarized as follows:

One day, a young man from Tokyo visited his friend in Nagano and saw a fire drill. All the villagers practiced putting out fires, as incidents of arson were being reported nightly. The strange thing was that the criminals had been already identified as Fujita Jūemon and an orphan girl, who was perhaps either his wife or daughter. Jūemon himself had suffered from a hernia since birth and his testicles were often swollen, which made him unable to run; for this reason, he was bullied at school. Although his parents did not really sympathize, Jūemon's grandparents loved him and took good care of him. However, after their deaths, Jūemon began to curse his parents for his disability and kicked them out of their house. He dilly-dallied in the village without finding a job and spent all the money he had. Soon his house was placed up for mortgage, which made him angry enough to set a fire in his neighborhood. Although caught and imprisoned, Jūemon was released six years later and he started gambling. Jūemon was imprisoned again for fraudulent practices, and after his second release, he started threatening his neighbors into giving him food. They were too terrified to resist and so he grew more selfish.

One day, Jūemon was so disturbed by his neighbors that he yelled at them, saying, "What's wrong with you? This village can't take care of even a single man like Jūemon! If you're too stingy to look after me, I don't need your help any more. I'll burn down this village!" After leaving, Jūemon lived with an orphan girl, and they began to burn down houses at random. Neither Jūemon nor the girl could be arrested, as Jūemon did not set the fires directly, while the girl was too quick to be caught. Whenever a house burned down, Jūemon came to deliver condolences to the victims; in accordance with custom, they had to offer him a cup of *sake* in return. He always drank a lot.

Finally, the villagers grew so fed up with him that they decided to drown him. The police and prosecutor were unable to identify the murderer. However, in the meantime, Jūemon's body was given to the girl, who put it on her back, walked to a hill, and cremated it all by herself. The villagers felt relieved, but when they fell asleep that night, the whole village turned into a sea of fire; the next morning, the burnt body of the girl was found.

The young man from Tokyo felt sympathy for Jūenom when he saw his body being taken out of the pond. Through this incident, he saw that Jūemon's innate nature had clashed with the norms of society, and he wept for his death. According to the man, happiness is gained when one's innate nature is fulfilled, but if each individual simply lived according to his own desire, society would become chaotic. Therefore rules are needed, and it is one's responsibility to observe them. Society develops as it enforces these laws, and law-making is the history and custom of human life. Society forces this acquired sense upon individuals, who must live in accordance with social laws. Once in a while, this acquired sense fails to control one's innate nature, and society regards this as breaking the law. The person who does this is labeled a criminal and discriminated against. For over six thousand years, people have succeeded in enforcing various laws by confronting their own innate natures; yet, the death of Jūemon indicates the shortcomings of this acquired sense and questions man's arrogance toward his own innate nature.

The young man cried to himself, "Defeat upon death! Jūemon's death is miserable. It shows the destiny of a natural child. However, in his defeat, isn't the quality of eternal life shown to us, as if a warrior were killed on the battlefield? Isn't he embraced in immeasurable life? Isn't tremendous sorrow shown in this event? Isn't there a need for humans to examine their way of life? From a much broader perspective, Jūemon was unique. People can fulfill their lives because they have a reason to live and talents to use. Therefore, Jūemon's life was never meaningless, even though he died like an animal without a proper funeral!" At the same time, the young man saw the villagers' innate natures in this incident. "Why did they kill Jūemon? How could their actions be justified? Were they not immoral? There must have been convulsions (uncontrollable innate natures) within them to provoke such a murder!"

Seven years after Jūemon's death, the young man heard that a grave for Jūemon and the girl were made at a temple, and that the villagers visited it regularly to make offerings to their spirits. He exclaimed, "Finally, the acquired sense returns to the innate nature!"

Yanagita regards innate nature as the source of bad action. To some extent, humanity itself is embraced in this nature, and all human activity is part of the landscape of this Earth. This perception is similar to that of biologists and natural historians, to whom man is merely one part of nature. In Yanagita's *Kainan shōki* (Travelogues), his sympathetic understanding for irrational human actions becomes apparent, while his observations on geographical aspects and communal life are read between the lines. Yanagita recorded all human activity objectively, seeing in it joy, anger, sorrow, and a longing for peace. Both the good and bad were embraced just as they were. Yanagita's perception is also applied to mentally and physically challenged people. For example, in *Yama no jinsei*, Yanagita writes:

The attitude towards mentally challenged people has
changed over the years. In the past, our ancestors thought
that children, full of imagination, sometimes became out of
control, stepped into an unknown world, and had unique
experiences.[5]

Another example is found in Yanagita's *Fukō naru geijutsu*
(Unfortunate Arts):

Until very recently, people living along the Japan Sea
coast took care of the mentally challenged very well. . .
for they thought that humans did not become foolish
easily.[6]

Yanagita wrote a separate chapter on so-called "unusual people"
in his *Sanson seikatsu no kenkyū* (The Study on the Lives in
Remote Mountains and Villages), discussing the dignity of both
the mentally and physically challenged. This perception was not
unique to him. Both unusual and ordinary events, or good and
bad occurrences, were accepted as parts of the landscape of
Mother Nature. Motoori Norinaga (1730-1801), a scholar of
Japanese classical literature and a pioneer of national learning
(*kokugaku*), shared Yanagita's vision. Any disturbing event was
caused by a vengeful deity called *Magatsuhi no kami*, who, when
angry, could not be stopped even by meritorious deities. In
essence, the majority of Japanese believed that they simply
needed to be patient and endure misfortunes until they passed;
there was no need to confront impermanence or look for the
meaning of life. This optimistic viewpoint is the basis for the
value of just being ordinary, which comes from the idea that time
eventually takes care of all problems.

The innate nature that Yanagita and Tayama pointed out
was viewed in the medieval period as karma (referring to one's
thoughts and acts and their corresponding consequences).
According to this way of thinking, inauspicious events were not
the result of a mere conflict between innate nature and society,
but rather, unwholesome karma was found in a person's innate
nature itself as an uncontrollable force that generated bad
conduct. This meant that self-confrontation was inevitable. As
everyone has to live with their own karma, which cannot be

separated from themselves, some people in those days sought consolation in revealed religion, and the teachings of Hōnen and Shinran answered their needs. In this sense, it must be remembered that the value of just being ordinary means avoiding any confrontation with one's own human nature.

4. Maintaining Balance

To understand the motivation to eliminate both good and bad elements from their communities, consider the analysis of Yamada Yoshihiko (1894-1975). He is also known as Kida Minoru, the scholar who introduced French philosophy to Japan by translating Fabre's *Souvenirs Entomologiques* and Durkheim's writings. Kida majored in sociology at the University of Paris and returned to Japan after World War II, where he lived in a small community (*buraku* or *mura*) west of Tokyo while observing Japanese life. [Translator's note: *buraku* in this context does not mean, as it often does, a residential area of people subjected to social discrimination.] Kida wrote two outstanding books, *Kichigai buraku shūyū kikō* (A Travelogue in Mad Communal Life), a novel satirizing postwar Japanese society, and *Nippon buraku* (A Collection of Sketches of Communal Life). The former won the Mainichi Publication Cultural Award in 1946; the latter was published in 1967 by Iwanami, a major Japanese publishing house. The features of communal life that Kida recorded were based on his own experiences in the *buraku* and may still be observed today, even though his analysis is out of date, as these communities started vanishing in the 1960s when Japan began to achieve remarkable economic growth.

In order to examine the communal life that Kida studied, *buraku* (*mura*) and *son* must first be explained, as *mura* and *son* have the same kanji character (村) and are often confused. *Buraku* refers to the basic community with its rules and customs, and in some cases, land put aside for the use of common welfare. Its formation occurred naturally through people having to live together. *Son* is the administrative town unit as defined by the law. ′

At the beginning of the Meiji period, there were more than

70,000 small communities, and according to Kida, cooperation was the most important feature in them. *Buraku* can be defined as a group of local residents learning how to live together with each other's help, without suppressing any individual opinion. This wisdom is called emotional "balancing" (*heikōka*), and Kida gave several concrete examples to support this.

For instance, if a person in a small community bought some rice for his family, other members would become jealous, avoid sharing in his happiness, and perhaps gossip that the person had become rich by gambling or doing some illegal work so that his filthy money would be wasted quickly. Again, when townspeople conveyed condolences to a family who lost someone, they would say, for example, that the family had once been very fortunate, but now they ran out of luck. Or a person might make fun of his neighbor who ate only pumpkins due to his poverty, even while he himself was merely eating potatoes every day. In short, by dealing with one's feelings in this way, the emotions of an entire community can be balanced.

Such balancing can be clearly seen in matters of material distribution. For instance, when trees were cut down and the branches cut off, the trunks were classified according to species, such as maple, ginkgo, zelkova, cedar, pine and oak, which were then stacked up and categorized by their combustibility. Although each pile weighed the same and was of the same quality, community members decided their portion by lottery because of their sensitivity to minor differences, including the size of the trunks and branches. This tedious work was necessary, as individuals were aware of their own greed. They also understood the meaning of interdependency among themselves even though fighting often occurred, and thus they strove to improve their communication with each other without holding back a single complaint. This process contributed to the development of wisdom within the community and reflected the way of thinking of those conducting the *saganagashi* ritual. Nevertheless, under these circumstances, communities tended to reject a person with strange ideas; Kida illustrates this in a story of the Zen priest Daikan.

Daikan resided at a poor temple three generations before Kida and would get up early every morning to chant sutras. He was liked very much by his community. He would preach to others about the importance of being honest with oneself and tell them that imitating others was unnecessary. Daikan taught his community to be aware of who they were in order to be at peace with themselves. As evidence of his conviction, he not only enjoyed gambling at the temple as part of fund-raising events, but he also took young men to bars and brothels. Although this upset others, Daikan continued to do so, reasoning that he was simply being honest. His moral views differed greatly from those of the average person, since Buddhism looks at worldly affairs from a spiritual perspective, though it was questionable whether Daikan taught this more subtle meaning to his community. Eventually, however, he was asked to leave because the people considered him dangerous and subversive, and disturbing their peace.

Both good and bad events were hindrances to a peaceful life in a small community; revealed religion was also rejected because, for the people living there, the only purpose of religion was to serve the entire community. This understanding is still dominant in society today and is one reason why the majority of the Japanese claim to be non-religious. Let us now look at this issue from another aspect.

5. The Value of Just Being Ordinary

As mentioned above, communities maintained harmony through understanding each other's needs, by which the bonds among one another were further developed. In other words, by balancing emotions and sharing material wealth equally among community members, harmony was kept. Each person was expected to examine his own behavior in relation to the others, and if something extraordinary were going to disturb the peace, the community would have to make sure that the damage would be kept to a minimum. The value of just being ordinary first appeared in the Kinki region (present-day Kyoto, Osaka, and Nara prefectures), and then spread throughout the country during the Tokugawa period, when small communities grew more economically independent.

According to Yanagita, the phenomenon also affected festivals (*matsuri*) and the concept of the deities tremendously, although in the medieval period, these divine beings were still regarded as transcendent. Yanagita's essay *Nihon no matsuri* (Festivals of Japan) describes the secularization of natural religion and Shinto, lowering both to the level of just being ordinary and contributing to the formation of today's non-religious climate. If spiritual perception and ordinary values were held on the same plane, religion would no longer be needed; the logic followed that it was perfectly all right to be non-religious.

During festivals in the medieval period, each participant had to stop his daily activities. However, according to Yanagita, three changes occurred in the Tokugawa period; 1) an increase in attendance of visitors; 2) a change in the religious motivation of parishioners of a community shrine (*ujiko*) holding the festivals (*matsuri*); and 3) the emergence of a professional ritual officiant.

As a result of the first change, festivals became merely cultural events and the custom of offering money at shrines grew popular. Festivals were originally held by local residents to enshrine their own community deities (*ujigami*), although on several islands of Okinawa, access during such events is still limited only to relatives and acquaintances of the residents.

On a more personal note, I tried to observe the *Yūkui* Festival on Miyakojima, one of the Okinawan islands, with my students in 1995. I had been making such requests since 1984, but they were always turned down. Although not allowed to attend, I was somewhat comforted to know that the tradition of restricting these events to local residents was still alive. On mainland Japan, such feelings concerning visitors are almost gone, and most festivals are seen merely as public community events.

As this kind of religious feeling decreased, the length of festivals was also affected. During the medieval period, festivals began at sunset and ended at dawn. Today, our day begins when the alarm clock rings (though such a lifestyle is relatively new, only having been brought to Japan during the Meiji period). In order to attract visitors, a portable shrine parades along the streets, and the climax of the festival is reached during midday. In Yanagita's opinion, these kinds of festivals are merely cultural events, though there are still quite a few religious ones kept according to tradition where, for example, a limited number of parishioners secretly perform rituals after midnight.

Yanagita states that after the custom of offering money in

boxes at shrines became widespread, the format of festivals changed drastically. Nowadays, these boxes are also found at Buddhist temples as well. The parishioners in the medieval period carried beautiful silk (*nusa*) on their travels and, when visiting shrines, offered it as a sign of their reverence. This silk was used instead of currency, but as time went by, people started giving money, thus beginning the modern tradition of an offertory box (*saisenbako*). As mentioned in Chapter 3, people originally worshiped two kinds of deities: those which had been enshrined by their descendants within their communities (*ujigami*), and those outside the communities. Offerings were made only to the former at the time of festivals. Nevertheless, the parishioner was accustomed to making offerings to deities outside his community, too. While prayers were made to ancestor deities, the parishioner started praying for personal wishes to other deities and offering money. According to Yanagita, this meant to challenge the deities and to personalize the faith shared by each community. At the *Aofushigaki* Festival held at Miho Shrine in Shimane prefecture, an officiant of the rituals, called *Tōya kannushi*, disciplined himself for three years in preparation. On behalf of his entire community, prayers to the *ujigami* were made for a large catch of fish, good harvest, and prosperity for the community. If one of the parishioners wished to pray personally, this had to be specially arranged with the officiant and performed privately. In the late 1960s, I filmed a Shinto festival at the Miho Shrine that was accompanied by music and the ritual prayer to the deity. During the festival, the officiant delivered a message to the deity, reporting on the amount of the annual harvest and any damage caused by natural disasters, details which concerned the whole community, without mentioning his own interests.

Hence, the custom of offering money brought about a new kind of prayer that reflected people's own personal desires and created new habits, such as continuously visiting shrines for a hundred days. In the people's mind, deities were static and would always be found at shrines; some people even thought that just by making one quick visit there, their personal wishes would be fulfilled. In the past, tremendous amounts of time were needed for the parishioners to unite with these deities, and festivals served as their means.

Although the personalization of faith, through making
personal wishes, contributed to the decline of the parishioner's
religious mind, another factor was involved, which was the
simplification of his religious practices. As mentioned in the
description of the *Aofushigaki* Festival, each parishioner had to
go through a long period of asceticism, which included
restricting one's diet, bathing in the ocean early in the morning
throughout the year, not traveling, refraining from sexual
intercourse, and not attending various meetings, after which time
a person would be ready to perform the certain rituals needed.

Some people inevitably abandoned these difficult
preparations, and alternative purification processes (*harai*) were
created. The most popular of these was *misogi*, in which one's
physical and spiritual defilements were removed by simply
taking a bath in the ocean or a river. This practice was further
simplified by merely washing one's hands and rinsing one's
mouth in a bowl (*chōzubachi*) before entering a shrine. Before
then, unless cleansed by water taken from the ocean or a river, no
parishioner was able to come in contact with the deities.
Simplification of the practices involved not only a shortening the
purification process, but also a continuation of ordinary life.

The third change was the appointment of full-time
officiants at local shrines. There are still a few shrines managed
by part-time priests who are chosen among residents by lottery or
requested from neighboring communities at the time of festivals.
At Miho Shrine, there are both full-time and part-time priests,
but the part-time priests (*Tōya kannushi*) have more power, as
the community nominates them to be in charge of the festival. In
the past, everyone within the community served the deities;
creating a position of professional ritual officiant was a sign of
declining religious concern for these celebrations.

In appointing bureaucrats to full-time priest positions, the
Meiji government took away the essence of natural religion. At
the same time, however, the decline of natural religion was
attributed to the attitude of the parishioners themselves. As
Yanagita states, after the seventeenth century people searched for
a way to continue ordinary life even during festival times; it is
clear that the value of just being ordinary contributed toward
such changes. If community members were to hold these
festivals for their own personal gain, it would indicate a

deterioration of their religious sensitivities, and the rituals would not be expressing their mutual interest.

6. Buddhist Teachings and the Value of Just Being Ordinary

Under the supervision of the family register system of the Tokugawa period, established Buddhist schools such as Tendaishū, Shingonshū, and Sōtōshū sought accommodation with lay members; originally, Buddhist teachings were reserved for monks and nuns pursuing of enlightenment. Other Buddhist sects, including Jōdoshū, Jōdoshinshū, and Nichirenshū also adopted structural changes in order to revive their declining membership. In this sense, Buddhist teachings were compromised as a reflection of the value of just being ordinary, and this is another factor contributing toward the non-religious climate of today.

Here I consider Suzuki Shōsan (1579-1655), a Sōtō Zen priest who first served Tokugawa Ieyasu as his warrior but later became ordained at the age of forty-two. Influenced by his samurai training, Suzuki's style of Zen was very strict. In one of his books, *Banmin tokuyō* (Virtue and Use for Everyone), he states that ordinary people could practice Buddhism in their own daily occupations; thus it was unnecessary for them to pray to Buddha, read sutras, or meditate in temples, unless these practices actually liberated people from their egos. According to Suzuki, a peasant should just chant the Nembutsu at each stroke of his plow, as this would make him focused; after taking care of the field, the peasant's land would become enriched, and nutritious vegetables would grow. Furthermore, for those who ate these vegetables, blind passions would disappear. Artisans and merchants could similarly practice Buddhism during their work. Suzuki thus explained the importance of practice pursued in everyday work, and he regarded traditional Buddhist training as pointless.

While Śākyamuni Buddha originally taught the Dharma to only monks and nuns, the Mahāyāna tradition, appearing approximately six hundred years after the Buddha's death, brought the teachings to lay people as well. According to Suzuki, the Buddhadharma as state law was a development of this tradition, as the law was aimed at ordinary people. Ordinary life was affirmed, and the achievement of Buddhahood was possible for a layperson without one having to leave his worldly life. Nevertheless, Suzuki's explanation needs to be analyzed, because those who agreed with him overlooked the true essence of the Buddha's teachings. Buddhism deals with the suffering and impermanence of life; becoming a buddha is not an affirmation of this ordinary life. Firstly, one needs to recognize how irrational life is; once this realization occurs, one's search for liberation can begin. Even after attaining enlightenment, a practitioner would still have to continue dealing with the impermanence of life.

According to Suzuki, Buddhist practices help one focus in battles. Does this mean that getting rid of blind passions contributes to the act of killing? He also said that the less one was concerned with fame and money, the better one's chances were of getting a decent job and promotion. Does that mean that teachings were implemented for one's own interest alone? Suzuki's general aim was to make daily activities more productive and run more smoothly; the Buddhist teachings served as the means for achieving this goal. Certainly, Buddhism teaches selflessness and liberation from the ego, which need to be achieved so that one's relationship with others can be improved. Nevertheless, controlling one's ego does not affirm an ordinary way of life. Contrary to Suzuki's position, Shin Buddhist tradition rejects the necessity of getting rid of the ego and obtaining any kind of practical merit.

During the Tokugawa period, mundane rules dominated, and Buddhism became merely moralistic and filial; the teachings failed to give a critical vision to the value of just being ordinary. The goal of revealed religion is to transcend daily problems of human life, and therefore the teachings and mundane rules should be well balanced (though a clash between the two is always possible).

The emphasis on the value of just being ordinary has affected not only natural religion and Buddhism but also Confucianism in Japan. For instance, Itō Jinsai, a scholar of Chinese Confucianism and the leader of Confucianism in Japan, degraded the Confucian teachings to the level of just being ordinary. Although Confucianism originally had a sense of transcendence and dealt with every single being on Earth, Itō's concern was limited to human relationships. To him, man could not live without truth, so it needed to be found within the realm of ordinary life. In other words, worldly life should be valued, as it was the only place where truth could be found.

The value of just being ordinary grew more popular after the seventeenth century and dominated Buddhism, Shinto, and Confucianism. Interestingly enough, this phenomenon had already been seen in China in the sixteenth century. According to Yo Eiji, various industries flourished there at that time because it was thought that truth was measured by one's performance in one's work; Confucians regarded the diligent for their wisdom. Was it coincidence that the value of just being ordinary gained popularity in China and Japan about the same time, despite minor differences between the make-up of both societies? This concurrence needs to be studied further.

Notes

1. "Saga." In *Nihon kokugo daijiten*. Tokyo: Shōgakkan, 1980.
2. Yanagita, Kunio. "Heibon to hibon." In *Teihon Yanagita Kunioshū 24.*
   Tokyo: Chikuma shobō, 1963, p.439.
3. Yanagita, "Nenchū gyōji oboegaki." In *Teihon Yanagita Kunioshū 13.*
   Tokyo: Chikuma shobō, 1963, p.90.
4. Yanagita, "Yama no jinsei." In *Teihon Yanagita Kunioshū 4.* Tokyo:
   Chikuma shobō, 1963, p.171.
5. Ibid., p.86.
6. Yanagita, "Fukō naru geijutsu." In *Teihon Yanagita Kunioshū 7.*
   Tokyo: Chikuma shobō, 1963, p.277.

Chapter 5

A Village Without Individual Graves

Today, many people participate in religious activities like visiting family graves, even if one is non-religious. Some Shinto priests who consider themselves non-religious also perform Shinto rites without difficulty within their own communities. In other words, the majority of people do not think about revealed religion when discussing such topics and the concepts of God and Buddha.

Of those who do not follow the custom of family grave visits, there appear to be two groups: devout Shin Buddhists, and the residents of Miyakojima in Okinawa prefecture. Shin Buddhists are practitioners of a revealed religion, while the Miyakojima residents are practitioners of a natural religion. Shin Buddhism was established in Southern and Western Japan (including Kyūshū, Chūgoku, and Kansai), Central Japan (Tōkai), and the Sea of Japan area (Hokuriku). Mainland Japanese accept that Shin Buddhists do not visit graves because of their particular teaching, but it is often difficult for mainland Japanese to understand why residents of Miyakojima do not visit family graves, as they belong to the same religion. By examining these two religious beliefs, we can better understand why changes within natural religion occurred.

1. Faith in *Uyagamu*

First, one must consider the physical dimensions of Japan.

The distance between Tokyo and Kagoshima by land and that between Miyakojima and Kagoshima by sea are about the same. In other words, if a straight line were to be drawn on a map between Tokyo and Miyakojima, Kagoshima would be located in the middle. The lands of Japan comprise vast amounts of water in the Pacific Ocean.

Miyakojima is the name of a whole island chain, of which one island called Miyakojima also exists in addition to four islands: Irabujima, Ikemajima, Kurimajima, and Ōgamijima. Ōgamijima, a cone-shaped island, is the smallest, with a circumference of less than three kilometers and only about twenty residents. From the scenic point at *Tonbaru* on the top of the island, the ocean can be viewed at 360 degrees, with Miyakojima in the south.

Although more than fifteen years have passed since I started visiting various islands in Okinawa, the Miyakojima chain is my favorite; whenever I go there, I stop by Ōgamijima.

On Ōgamijima and in the small communities of Karimata and Shimajiri on Miyakojima, the Festival of *Uyagamu* is held, which is named after the island's female residents who are selected to perform this ritual sometime between October and December (depending on the lunar calendar). Visitors and anthropologists are not allowed to attend this and other ceremonies, as they are considered intruders and would violate local taboos and disrespect various deities. In Yanagita's words, this is for the sake of the community, as these festivals are not simply cultural events. The residents on Ōgamijima are successful in preserving the sanctity of these festivals; visitors arrive by ship and so can be stopped, whereas in Karimata and Shimajiri, there is access through neighboring communities.

On a more personal note, one day I boarded a ship with my students without realizing that it was that particular time of the year. But recognizing me from an earlier trip, the captain took us to the island anyway. Nevertheless, we were stopped after landing. I felt ashamed for ignoring the captain's feelings and not contacting the residents of the island beforehand. Although we were turned away, this experience helped my students to truly understand the sacredness of the festival. The captain reasoned that if the residents of Ōgamijima became friendly with visitors and researchers, they could benefit financially, but tradition overruled his opinion. Even though his community was poor as a result of this policy, it could not be helped. If I were in the captain's position, I would have done the same thing. For this personal experience, I hope that the reader can recognize the true sanctity of natural religion.

After that incident, I stopped directly asking the residents of Miyakojima about the festival and instead inquired about their lifestyle, which seemed to inspire my students, as they did not know very much about Japanese culture other than their own lives in Tokyo. Nevertheless, the Ōgamijima residents often mentioned the festival and I had many opportunities to hear about it after getting to know them well. Then, after seeing part of the ceremony held in Karimata, I was able to describe it roughly myself. I strongly feel that the spirituality found in the *Uyagamu* Festival is so deep that the true religious feelings of natural religion can even be felt by the totally non-religious (even though my attempt to discuss it here may violate Ōgamijima tradition, which prohibits its residents from propagating the festival to strangers).

On Ōgamijima, no cemetery is found except for two or three crypts built on the coast, which have been constructed recently and are quite different from those on mainland Japan. Each is made of cement, rectangular in shape, and is big enough to accommodate two or three adults; its entrance is sealed up with plaster. The people of Okinawa once let dead bodies naturally decompose by placing them in caves along the coast for a certain period, after which time people would wash the bones, put them in jars, and then return them to the same caves. These were never visited again until there was another death. However, influenced by customs on mainland Japan, the people in Okinawa began to move the jars to another location, where crypts began being built. However, the local people hardly visit these graves, and one cannot find any offerings of flowers or incense there.

In the tradition of Okinawa, all deceased are believed to become deities and their spirits are enshrined right after death, so that the people in Okinawa are not really attached to the dead. For them, a body without a spirit is no good to anyone. Even the custom of enshrining spirits was unnecessary, as death meant instant elevation to the state of deity. Nevertheless, at a time when mainland Japan greatly valued funeral and memorial services, through which the deceased became *hotoke*, people in Okinawa began to believe that the spirit would gradually become deity; thus, they started honoring spirits. Today on Ōgamijima, a Buddhist priest occasionally officiates at funerals, but the customs of performing memorial services and visiting graves have never been widespread there.

Also, on mainland Japan the spirits of the deceased were enshrined in a two-part ceremony system (*ryōbosei*) composed of a burial or cremation and then rituals or offerings to honor the spirits. The Japanese were once not attached to the bodies of the deceased; today, influenced by humanistic feelings, they have become obsessed with how to deal with human ashes, for example whether to scatter them in nature or place them in graves. Some people even purchase their own grave plots while they are still alive! This phenomenon merely shows the decline of the religious mind and, in fact, of natural religion itself.

There is another reason that the residents of Ōgamijima remain faithful to natural religion. They have always respected the deities of fire, their houses, and the tutelary deity called *Mau*, more than the spirits of their ancestors. Among these divines, *Uyagamu* is the greatest, as he is said to have fallen from heaven. The dates honoring this deity and other ancestral spirits differ, with the latter being celebrated only on the sixteenth of February.

Recently, I had the chance to hear about a spiritual journey made by a resident of Ōgamijima. He told me that after moving to the mainland of Okinawa, he worked as a laborer at the U.S. military base; his life had been very difficult, but he never lost faith in *Uyagamu*. Since childhood, the man had taken it for granted that the deity would protect him under any circumstances, so he did not feel responsible for his life. One day, however, his wife criticized him for his conduct and he realized then that he had always been looking for the easy way out. He started taking responsibility for himself after that point. Nevertheless, it took him a long time to understand why he needed to entrust himself in *Uyagamu*. He occasionally prayed to the deity for his hardships to be removed, but finally he came to realize that the *Uyagamu* had already spiritually embraced him, even though nothing special happened in his life. This transformation showed the man's awareness of religion, which was very different from his own ordinary values.

This story reminds me of the Ōmi merchants of the eighteenth century (*Ōmi shōnin*; Ōmi is in present-day Shiga prefecture). They made a great deal of money as devout Shin Buddhist; the merchants entrusted in Amida Buddha that they would become also buddhas after death. They did not pray for their success in business, but rather worked hard and were practical in daily life and in dealing with everyday problems. Although the person I met on Ōgamijima was not as successful as these merchants, his religious viewpoint changed after he had found spirituality in *Uyagamu* and as his responsibilities for himself became clearer. The residents on that island are more spiritually enriched than the non-religious people on mainland Japan, who often pray to deities for success and luck in life.

While faith in *Uyagamu* is limited to Ōgamijima, entrusting in Amida Buddha occurs throughout Japan. Nevertheless, both figures help people establish their own spirituality within the realm of transcendence. The island residents do not need revealed religion and criticize the propagation of new beliefs. They also do not believe in shamans (*yuta*) or magical amulets such as shells shaped in the kanji character for water (*suijigai*), which are used for physical protection. In like manner, the devout Shin Buddhists are also free from superstition.

Despite identifying themselves as non-religious, the residents of Ōgamijima are well aware of their own traditions; this so-called title applies only to their lack of belief in revealed religion.

2. Entrusting Oneself in the Teaching in a Traditional Paper-Making Village

In the village community of Yamane, there are no individual graves, even at the local temple. One day, I asked the resident priest about this; he showed me a small stone monument on the right-hand side, immediately after entering the temple's main gate, on which the six letters of Namu-Amida-Butsu were inscribed. Behind this was a large stone covering a hole, into which local people threw the ashes of all the dead. This served as their communal grave, and the inscription on the monument was the only sign indicating where it was.

Many people in cities quarrel over how they wish to be buried or how their relatives should be buried; for instance, the ashes of such and such individuals should not be buried together as they did not get along well in life; some parents and children do not want to share the same gravesite, and so on. For these people, the concept of having a communal burial place would be unthinkable, like living with total strangers. Nevertheless, sharing a grave seems rational to me, as it does not require as much space as individual burials and, best of all, it avoids the conflicts mentioned above.

The town of Yamane is located in Aoyachō in Tottori prefecture (in the west, on the Sea of Japan) and its local temple is Ganshōji. This village has been known for two things: its traditional handmade paper (*washi*) made mainly from mulberry bark (*kouzo*), and its devout Shin Buddhists. Hence, it was the Shin Buddhist understanding of the teaching which has kept alive the Yamane custom of communal burial.

The life of Ashikaga Genza (1842-1930) is introduced in the rest of this chapter. Genza was a devout Shin Buddhist who became well known after Yanagi Muneyoshi (1889-1961), the pioneer of the folk crafts' movement, wrote about him in *Myōkōnin Inaba no Genza* (The Biography of Devout Genza in Inaba region). *Myōkōnin* literally means "pure white lotus" (Skt. *puṇḍarīka*) blooming in the mud; the lotus represents devout followers who entrust themselves in Amida Buddha while acknowledging their blind passions. In the second half of the Tokugawa period, people were interested in the lives of such devout Shin Buddhists, who were often poor and uneducated. Many books describing their lives were published, and Yanagi's contribution was a modern-day revival of *Myōkōnin*.

Genza, who lived his entire life in Yamane, was a peasant working in the local *washi* industry. At the age of eighteen he lost his father, which was a crisis point for him. The story describes the crisis: One early morning in August, Genza and his father were working in a paddy-field harvesting rice, when the father suddenly became sick. Upon returning home that night, he passed away. His last words to Genza were to entrust himself in *oyasama*, which would bring about a spiritual awakening in him. At that moment, Genza did not know what to do, how he could find *oyasama*, and why he should even try.

While it is natural for people to think about the meaning of life in general and to have various questions after experiencing the death of someone close, for Shin Buddhists, the answer is found in *oyasama*. Since the medieval period, they have called Amida Buddha *oyasama*, literally meaning "parent." Even today, some people also call Buddha *nonosama*, and according to Orikuchi Shinobu, this means "mother." By personifying Amida Buddha as *oyasama*, Shin Buddhists have associated spiritual compassion with a mother's embrace.

Genza knew all of this, but he could not feel Amida's compassion. He began to visit Ganshōji, as his father used to go there to listen to the teaching and to question the priest about *oyasama*. However, it took Genza twelve years to understand such compassion; this experience came suddenly when he was thirty, after which Genza was finally able to entrust himself in Amida Buddha. It is said that one day, he went to a nearby hill with his cow to bring home some grass. Genza carried the heavy load on his shoulder, as he felt sorry for his cow, but eventually he became tired and decided to put it on his cow's back. At that moment, Genza experienced a kind of conversion as he was instantly relieved, and through this he felt Amida's compassion.

He had been desperate for such compassion, as his father had pointed out to him. After his father's death, Genza was very lonely, and this had conditioned him to look for spiritual peace. Genza sought Amida's compassion, for without it, the search for *oyasama* would have been meaningless. However, Genza could not figure out for a long time how to rely on Amida, as he was ignorant of his own limitations. People often behave rightly in order to receive physical protection from deities, after which their faith develops in exchange for benefits given to them by these deities. Before experiencing his conversion, Genza was also concerned about merit-making and disciplining himself, thinking that someday Amida Buddha would embrace him for his good actions. However, this could not work, as Amida Buddha made vows solely to liberate all sentient beings from the realm of birth and death as long as they called his Name. In other words, the act of calling Buddha's name together with an entrusting mind (*shinjin*) in the teaching was the only necessary requirement for birth in the Pure Land; all other practices were secondary. Needless to say, the uttering of the Nembutsu did not liberate Genza right away, as it was merely mechanical, and his religious consciousness needed further development.

Genza had continued to listen to the teaching for more than ten years after his father's death, but he only understood the importance of the Nembutsu intellectually. He did not realize the true nature of his own ego. Although Amida's compassion is immeasurable, the human mind limits its understanding; for example, individuals often use the Nembutsu for their own purposes, such as reciting it ten thousand times a day or saying it just once. Every effort should be made to understand Amida Buddha and even to confront him as one seeks truth, since there is something about the concept of transcendence that people doubt. When individuals come to realize their limitations, they are able to awaken to the compassion of Amida Buddha, who takes pity on them and embraces them as they are. From that point on, this compassion is no longer questioned; human beings, unable to entrust themselves to anything other than themselves, develop a standpoint within the realm of transcendence.

Genza, for example, had become tired of carrying the grass but was instantly relieved after putting it on the back of his cow. This ordinary experience turned his mind, as he had been searching for Amida's compassion at a much deeper level.

3. The Turning of the Mind: Conversion

While revealed religion requires conversion, natural religion does not. Through annual events such as *obon* and New Year's celebrations or by participating in local festivals, people generally come to respect local deities and worship their ancestors naturally; a strong, conscious choice to follow religion does not arise among them.

There are two types of conversions: dramatic, as in Genza's case, or gradual. Those raised in a family belonging to a congregation tend to participate in religious events from birth, so they gradually come to understand the teachings of revealed religion. Without knowing anything about conversion, those who gradually turned their mind are able to differentiate between their current spiritual lives and lives that they had before the conversion.

I met an old man in Yamane about thirty years ago who told

me that he had finally come to appreciate a passage from Shinran in the *Tannishō* (A Record in Lament of Divergences) which states: "When I [Shinran] consider deeply the Vow of Amida, which arose from five kalpas [immeasurable time] of profound thought, I realize that it was entirely for the sake of myself alone! Then how I am filled with gratitude for the Primal Vow, in which Amida resolved to save me, though I am burdened with such heavy karma."[1] Although his conversion was not as dramatic as Genza's, this man was able to realize the true essence of Shin Buddhism by listening constantly to the teaching for more than thirty years.

The importance of conversion is not to know when one is actually converted, but to identify the point when one is confronted by the meaning of life and other spiritual questions. Changes in one's daily life and a new spiritual awareness after the conversion are also essential to this process. I am addressing this because revealed religion is often misunderstood as performing mysterious rites, and psychological changes in the followers are reported. Is it true, then, that one must have a mystical experience in order to convert to any teachings?

One day, I spoke to an old Rinzai Zen master about a unique experience of Soga Ryōjin (1875-1971), a prominent scholar of Shin Buddhism and a priest of Higashi Honganji. I told the master that when Soga was reciting the Nembutsu in front of the figure of Amida Buddha, it suddenly disappeared, and instead a bodhisattva emerged. When Soga turned around, he saw another bodhisattva standing behind him, to which he himself was praying. After this, Soga saw many sets of this bodhisattva and himself. Soga used the Buddhist teachings to reflect upon his unusual experience and recalled that the vows of the bodhisattvas were made to liberate all sentient beings from suffering, and so he understood that he had benefited from countless lives in the past, present, and future. In other words, sentient beings were meant to live a life of interdependency, which is the basis of all life. After listening to my story, the Zen master replied that it was important for Soga to know himself in relation to all other beings, but not to see many sets of bodhisattvas and himself in such a mystical way.

In focusing on their minds, practitioners often experience such events after which they think that they are enlightened. For this reason, Zen masters supervise practitioners, and the actual practice of Zen prevents them from having illusions of enlightenment. Understanding the Buddhist teachings at each level of practice is more important than mastering mystical experiences.

In our earlier case of Genza, his dramatic conversion was less important than his understanding of the Other Power (the compassion of Amida Buddha) and his new spiritual life. He saw several changes in himself afterwards; the most significant among them was his statement that "everything in this world becomes true." Genza realized that, although he was assured of becoming a buddha in the future through Amida's Primal Vow, he still was a demon, due to his ignorance and greed in daily life. Genza was able to accept his entire life and realized who he truly was. This kind of spiritual understanding is essential for human beings, who often make judgments from their own limited viewpoints, turn away from problems in which they are involved, and accept only what they like as real in life. Owing to his transformation, Genza confronted his misfortunes head-on and dealt with them sincerely and spontaneously. One's ability to accept life as it is means being flexible and open-minded to whatever happens. This can be referred to as "the single path free of hindrances" described in the *Tannishō*, as opposed to being passive, stubborn, or stuck in one's own traditional ways.[2] The Nembutsu practitioners are able to live confidently even in the midst of hardships, because Amida Buddha's compassion has filled their hearts.

Actually, Genza faced many hardships in his life, including the loss of two sons. His first son became mentally ill at the age of twenty-one, after losing the son's daughter and his paddy-fields due to a natural disaster. Although Genza's first son recovered from this, he passed away when he was forty-nine, after which Genza's second son, in Kyoto, began suffering from a mental problem as well. Genza brought him back to Yamane and took care of him until he died. Genza understood that these events resulted from what is known as the Dependent Co-Arising (*innen*), and thus he appreciated Amida Buddha's compassion even more.[3]

Genza hardly lost his temper because of his natural humbleness, though having *shinjin*, entrusting mind, definitely helped him to be kind and patient. According to Genza, one became angry when one's pride was hurt, but he had nothing to be proud of. Amida Buddha had felt pity for him and endured his hardships on his behalf, so, Genza was able to free himself from his own problems, and thus there was no need for anger. Genza often helped others in difficulty by carrying heavy items for the elderly, taking care of the sick, giving his neighbors fertilizer for their fields, and paying taxes on behalf of the poor. Despite volunteering in these ways, which often went unnoticed, he never bragged about himself. Genza also took care of animals; once he calmed a bull by massaging him all night and telling him stories about *oyasama*.

Genza was a hard-working man who got up at one or two o'clock in the morning each day. He chanted the *Shōshinge* (Hymn of True Shinjin and the Nembutsu) composed by Shinran, made five or six straw sandals, and then left to the field to cut grass with his cow before dawn.[4] He never lit a fire at home even in winter, as Amida's compassion kept him warm, nor did he talk about the weather or other small matters when greeting people. He did not enjoy drinking or smoking but took genuine pleasure in helping others and giving them massages, for doing so gave him a chance to talk about Amida Buddha.

Genza was probably a naturally disciplined person. (He had already received an award from the local government at the age of nineteen.) His virtue and great personality developed as he entrusted in the Shin Buddhist teaching. Nevertheless, it is not my intention to praise Genza as a charismatic person or stress the wondrous effects of having *shinjin*. I also refuse to accept that one becomes invulnerable to misfortunes after spiritual transformation, as one's personality and lifestyle does not change easily. As the Japanese proverb says, "a person never changes his appearance unless cremated."

It is not necessarily the role of religion to create a better person, and one should not try to find compassion only through this. Even those who lack religion may be humble, while those who follow religion can still be arrogant. Also, these people may express sorrow when disturbed by unexpectedly difficult events. Even at the time of Hōnen, *shinjin* was seen by some as a kind of magic that made a person happy. Hōnen tried to explain that entrusting in the Nembutsu teaching was very different from being sensational or spectacular, as we can read below:

> After being able to entrust in the teaching, some people feel
> like bouncing between heaven and earth due to their
> infatuation in it; then their bodies become like goose-flesh
> and cry. Nevertheless, this state of mind merely describes
> their excitement and has nothing to do with their having
> *shinjin.* Entrusting in the teaching means that their doubts
> in Amida Buddha's wisdom and compassion have been
> removed.[5]

When the true intent of Amida's Primal Vow is understood, one's
heart is filled with joy, though *shinjin* itself may be felt quietly.
Experiencing rapture is not the only factor in determining the
state of one's conversion. If human beings could easily obtain
firm and settled faith, religion would be unnecessary;
unfortunately, as the mind is hard to control, there is always a
need for religion.

After his father passed away, Genza asked himself in what
he was truly to entrust himself, and gradually Genza realized that
spirituality was found in the compassion of Amida Buddha,
which transcends all one's understanding. Through this
compassion, one can learn about oneself even in difficult
situations and learn to practice compassion. For Genza,
"everything in this world becomes true," a realization that shows
the depth of his spirituality and which can never be gained
through an academic study of morality and metaphysics.

When he was about to die at the age of eighty-nine,
Genza's long-time friend asked him how he could entrust himself
in Amida's compassion too. Genza's reply was very simple:
Oyasama had already begun to embrace him, and therefore all he
had to do was to die naturally and he would be in the hands of
Amida. It was unnecessary to try to understand what this
compassion was. In the early morning of February 20, 1930,
Genza died while uttering the Nembutsu; his friend passed away
the next day.

The town of Yamane has had many devout Shin Buddhists;
it is known for its unique religious climate nurturing spirituality,
and is known as "the soil of virtue" (*dotoku*). In December 1995,
I received a postcard from a person living in Yamane whom I had

known for a long time. He had learned about the beauty of folk
crafts from Yanagi Muneyoshi and had succeeded in developing
a method of mass production in the *washi* industry. This man was
also a devout Shin Buddhist and a successor to Genza's tradition.
On various occasions, he taught me the essence of Shin
Buddhism and about the folk crafts' movement, which he
practiced in his daily life. If the search for spirituality begins
with meeting such a religious person, my spiritual journey started
with him. His postcard thanked me for the condolences I
delivered to him when his third son passed away. On the front of
the card, two kanji characters of *dotoku* were written, and he
wrote, "Even intolerable misfortune is absorbed into the soil of
virtue, where the devout are encouraged to appreciate their lives.
Everyone is fine!" On the back was Genza's favorite saying,
"Welcome and welcome [to Amida's wondrous world]" (*yōkoso
yōkoso*). I was very happy to see the religious climate of the
myōkōnin being kept in the countryside and I wanted to share
this depth of revealed religion with the people in Tokyo.

Being part of a congregation, belonging to a revealed
religion, does not mean that everyone has to experience a
dramatic conversion. In fact, some gradually change after
attending services continuously over several years, and ironically,
those who have not yet had such an experience contribute largely
to the maintenance of the religious institution. Following this
logic, there are two kinds of people: those who need to be
converted and those who do not. William James labeled the
former as "sick souls" and the latter as possessing "healthy-
mindedness":

> The sufferer, when saved, is saved by what seems to him a
> second birth, a deeper kind of conscious being than he
> could enjoy before.[6]

> The completest religions would therefore seem to be those
> in which the pessimistic elements are best developed.
> Buddhism, of course, and Christianity are the best known to
> us of these. They are essentially religions of deliverance:
> the man must die to an unreal life before he can be born
> into the real life.[7]

Healthy-minded people do not question human existence or see
their lives being full of irrationality; rather, they see that this
world is in harmony and filled with beauty. A so-called merciful
God never makes demands upon healthy-minded individuals. For
these reasons, they do not regret their mistakes in the past, and
instead believe in courage, hope, and trust while ignoring fear,
worry, and doubt. Happiness is part of their being; it is
unnecessary for these believers to have a conversion experience.
They are people who are "once-born," as it were. On the other
hand, those with a sick soul perceive their lives anxiously and
see unhappiness in human nature. They are worried about
impermanence, yearn to discover the meaning of life, and seek
spiritual liberation. Such people need to be "born again" in a
spiritual sense to experience religion.

Since both types of belief tend to intertwine, the spiritual
hunger of each individual is different. Some people need to have
such an experience while others do not, even though the
experience may be tied to revealed religion.

Aside from the theme of this book, why Japanese lack
religious beliefs, it can be said that the great majority of them are
"healthy-minded." They can be comforted by James' observation
that "the best repentance is to up and act for righteousness, and
forget that you ever had relations with sin."[8] Does this mean that
revealed religion, which demands conversion, is unsuitable for
the healthy-minded climate of Japan? It should not be forgotten
that Japan has also enjoyed the twice-born culture in the form of
Shin Buddhism and its teaching on ego and karma. Politicians
and intellectuals in Tokyo have become ignorant of their own
spiritual roots after Japan's historical entrance into modernity.
Today, unbeknownst to these cynics, devout people like Genza
can be found throughout Japan. The possibility of restoring their
religious mind to the Japanese majority is still present.

In discussing Genza's life, I hope I have allowed the reader
to observe the spiritual quality of revealed religion, apart from
non-religious tradition. The Japanese religious mind cannot
simply be deemed non-religious, due to the paradoxical
expressive nature of spiritual feelings as described above. What
is important for us now is to understand our religious minds in a
proper historical setting. This historical religious education must
be carried out accurately and deliberately; otherwise, we shall

fail to understand not only our own people and culture, but also the development of comparative Japanese studies in relation to other countries.

Notes

1. The *Tannishō* is greatly respected in the Shin Buddhist tradition, although Shinran did not write this. It was complied by his direct follower, said to be Yuien, who crystallized Shinran's teaching and corrected misunderstandings that circulated among followers immediately after Shinran's death. See Hirota, Dennis, ed. and trans. et al, *The Collected Works of Shinran,* vol.1. Kyoto: Jōdo Shinshū Hongwanji-ha, 1997, p.679. [Translator's note]

2. "The nembutsu is the single path free of hindrances. Why is this? To practicers who have realized shinjin, the gods of the heavens and earth bow in homage, and maras and nonbuddhists present no obstruction. No evil act can bring about karmic results, nor can any good act equal the nembutsu." Ibid., p.665. [Translator's note]

3. Dependent Co-Arising (Skt: *pratītya-samutpāda*) is what Śākyamuni Buddha discovered in his awakening, and is the analysis of one's attachment to samsāra and at the same time spiritual liberation. Dependent co-arising and Dharma are seen as equivalent. By realizing the patterns of cause and effect within one's own existence, the problem of suffering can be explained, leading one to attainment of nirvana. See Robinson, Richard and Willard Johnson. *The Buddhist Religion: A Historical Introduction,* 4th ed. Belmont: Wadsworth Publishing, 1997, pp.23-9. [Translator's note]

4. *Shōshinge* consists of one hundred and twenty lines in sixty verses. It is found at the end of the second volume in *Ken jōdo shinjitsu kyōgyōshō monrui,* better known as the *Kyōgyōshinshō* ("The True Teaching, Practice, and Realization of the Pure Land Way"), which is Shinran's magnum opus. The *Shōshinge* has two parts: an explanation of the teaching, and a praise of the Seven Masters of the Pure Land teaching, who are Nāgārjuna and Vasubandhu in India; T'an-luan, Tao-ch'o, and Shan-tao in China; and Genshin and Hōnen in Japan. The *Shōshinge* is widely chanted in various Shin Buddhists' services. See *The Collected Works of Shinran,* vol. 1, pp.69-74. [Translator's note]

5. Hōnen. "Ōjōdaiyōshō." In *Jōdoshū seitein: Shōwa shinsan kokuyaku daizōkyō,* edited by Kyōdō Ishii. Tokyo: Tōhō shoin, 1928, p.113.

6. James, William. *The Varieties of Religious Experience.* New York: Penguin Books, 1985, p.157.

7. Ibid., p.165.

8. Ibid., p.127.

Epilogue

In a 1996 issue of the *Asahi Shinbun,* a Japanese national newspaper, there was an article about a person riding on the railway without a train ticket, and a corresponding comment from a reader who said that most Japanese are not disciplined enough as they are not very religious and particularly lack Christian ideals. I was shocked to read that riding illegally had something to do with the Japanese religious mind! Nevertheless, this is a common belief of not only the majority of Japanese intellectuals but also the ordinary people, that their spiritual lives are non-religious.

In 1903, a Japanese magazine called *Dōbō* carried an interesting article that had been widely circulated at the beginning of the nineteenth century in Hawaii, whose title was "The Japanese Empire made up of monkey-men and the Japanese people who do not have religion" (*saru no hitomane shitaru nihon teikoku to mushūkyō no nihon kokumin*). Naturally, such an expression would make sense in those days as it was presented from within the Christian tradition. However, even among the Japanese people in the nineteenth century, non-religiousness was already prevalent. In 1893, Fukuzawa Yukichi (the founder of Keiō University in Tokyo) had written an article entitled "The main family producing non-religious leaders" (*mushūkyōka seizō no honke*).

It amazes me that the majority of the Japanese people have either avoided (or favored) the word "non-religious" for more than a hundred years, which I think is very strange and even appalling. I believe that religion, not only Christianity but also organized Japanese Buddhism, gives us a fundamental perspective on life and that this perspective starts only when we truly realize our own limitations. There must be some reason why so many Japanese have avoided participating in organized religion.

In this book, I have described two types of Japanese religious histories: the development of the Japanese religious mind from the Meiji period to the present day, and the cultural and ethnic influences of natural religion, which runs more deeply and continuously as a structure. In writing this book, I realized that the Japanese religious mind is much more complicated and has deeper roots than I had previously imagined. Nevertheless, I hope that this exploration will contribute in some way to the study of Japanese religious culture.

Ama, Toshimaro
August 26, 1996

Bibliography

Aihara, Ichirōsuke. "Yakugo Shūkyō no seiritsu." In *Shūkyōgaku kiyō*, vol. 5 (1938): pp. 4-5.

Ama, Toshimaro. *Yanagi Sōetsu: Bi no bosatsu.* Tokyo: Libropōto, 1987.

―――. *Hōnen no shōgeki: Nihon bukkyō no radical.* Kyoto: Jinbun shoin, 1989.

―――. *Kokka shugi o koeru: Kindai nihon no kenshō.* Tokyo: Kōdansha, 1994.

―――. *Shūkyō no shinsō: Sei naru mono e no shōdō.* Tokyo: Chikuma gakugei bunko, 1995.

Aruga, Kizaemon. *Hitotsu no nihon bunkaron.* Tokyo: Miraisha, 1976.

Ashizu, Uzuhiko. *Kokka Shinto to wa nan dattanoka.* Tokyo: Jinja shinpōsha, 1987.

Bitō, Masahide. *Edo jidai to wa nanika.* Tokyo: Iwanami shoten, 1992.

Fujii, Kenshi. "Meiji shoki ni okeru Shinshū no Shintokan." In *Tokyō gakugei daigaku kiyō*, daini bumon 39 (1988): pp. 147-56.

Hashimoto, Mineo. *Ukiyo no shisō.* Tokyo: Kōdansha, 1975.

Hikaku Shisōshi Kenkyūkai. *Meiji shisōka no shūkyōkan.* Tokyo: Daizō shuppan, 1975.

Hōnen. "Ōjōdaiyōshō." In *Jōdoshū seiten: Shōwa shinsan kokuyaku daizōkyō*, edited by Kyōdō Ishii. Tokyo: Tōhō shoin, 1928.

Inoue, Kowashi. "Gaikyō seigen ikenan." In *Inoue Kowashiden: Shiryōhen 1*, edited by Inoue Kowashi Denki Hensan Iinkai. Tokyo: Kokugakuin daigaku toshokan, 1969.

―――. "Kyōdōshoku haishi ikenan." In *Inoue Kowashiden: Shiryōhen 1*, edited by Inoue Kowashi Denki Hensan Iinkai. Tokyo: Kokugakuin daigaku toshokan, 1969.

―――. "Ōshū mohō o arazu to suru setsu." In *Inoue Kowashiden: Shiryōhen 1*, edited by Inoue Kowashi Denki Hensan Iinkai. Tokyo: Kokugakuin daigaku toshokan, 1969.

————. "Yamagata sangi shūkyō shobun ikenan." In *Inoue Kowashiden: Shiryōhen 6*, edited by Inoue Kowashi Denki Hensan Iinkai. Tokyo: Kokugakuin daigaku toshokan, 1977.

Ishida, Ichirō. "Hayashi Razan no shisō." In *Fujiwara Seika to Hayashi Razan: Nihon shisōshi taikei 28*. Tokyo: Iwanami shoten, 1975.

Itō, Hirobumi. *Kenpō gikai*. Tokyo: Iwanami shoten, 1940.

Iwanami kogo jiten. Tokyo: Iwanami shoten, 1974.

Izumi, Shigeki. "Takagi Kenmyōshi no jiseki ni tsuite." In *Shindō*, vol.14 (1995): pp. 59-81.

————. "Takagi Kenmyō no gyōjitsu." In *Shinshū*, (March 1996): pp.63-9.

James, William. *The Varieties of Religious Experience*. Translated by Keizaburō Masuda. Tokyo: Nihon kyōbunsha, 1962.

Japan: An Illustrated Encyclopedia. Tokyo: Kōdansha, 1993.

"Jinkan yūshi jingikan secchi chinjōsho." In *Shūkyō to Kokka: Nihon kindai shisō taikei 5*, edited by Masato Miyaji and Yoshio Yasumaru. Tokyo: Iwanami shoten, 1988.

Kanzaki, Nobutake. *Inaka kannushi funsenki*. Tokyo: Kōdansha, 1991.

Karaki, Junzō. *Mujō*. Tokyo: Chikuma shobō, 1964.

Kashiwabara, Yūsen. "Buke kakun ni okeru jukyō juyō no katei." In *Nihon kinsei kindai bukkyōshi no kenkyū*, edited by Yūsen Kashiwabara. Kyoto: Heirakuji shoten, 1969.

————. "Gohō shisō to shomin kyōka." In *Kinsei bukkyō no shisō: Nihon shisō taikei 57*, edited by Manabu Fujii and Yūsen Kashiwabara. Tokyo: Iwanami shoten, 1973.

Kida, Minoru. *Kichigai buraku shūyū kikō*. Tokyo: Fusanbō, 1981.

————. *Nippon buraku*. Tokyo: Iwanami shoten, 1967.

Kinugasa, Isshō and Muneyoshi Yanagi, eds. *Myōkōnin Inaba no Genza*. Kyoto: Hyakkaen, 1960.

Kumazawa, Banzan. "Shūgiwasho." In *Kumazawa Banzan: Nihon shisō taikei 30*, edited by Ryūtarō Tomoeda and Yōichi Gotō. Tokyo: Iwanami shoten, 1971.

Matsuda, Osamu. "Kōshoku ichidai otoko e no michi." In *Kōshoku ichidai otoko*. Tokyo: Shinchōsha, 1982.

Mishima, Ryōchū. *Kakushō hiroku Kōson shōnin ketsuruiki*. Tokyo: Showa shuppansha, 1929.

Mori, Ryūkichi. *Shinran so no shisōshi.* Tokyo: Sanichi shobō, 1961.

Nakajima, Sachio. "Dainippon teikoku kenpō dai nijūhachijō, shinkō jiyū kitei seiritsu no zenshi." In *Nihonshi kenkyū,* vol. 168 (1976): pp. 1-32.

Nihon kokugo daijten. Tokyo: Shōgakkan, 1980.

Nishi, Amane. "Kyōmonron." In *Nishi Amane zenshū 1,* edited by Toshiaki Ōkubo. Tokyo: Shūkō shobō, 1962.

Nishi, Sawanosuke. "Shinto wa shūkyō ni arazaru no ron." In *Shūkyō to Kokka: Nihon kindai shisō taikei 5,* edited by Masato Miyaji and Yoshio Yasumaru. Tokyo: Iwanami shoten, 1988.

Ōno, Shinya, ed. *Iwanami kogo jiten.* Tokyo: Iwanami shoten, 1974.

Shimaji, Mokurai. "Sanjō bengi." In *Shimaji Mokurai zenshū 1,* edited by Hirotaka Fukushima and Kenkō Futaba. Kyoto: Honganji shuppan kyōkai, 1973.

———. "Daikyōin bunri kenpakusho." In *Shimaji Mokurai zenshū 1,* edited by Hirotaka Fukushima and Kenkō Futaba. Kyoto: Honganji shuppan kyōkai, 1973.

Shinshū Kyōgaku Kenkyūsho. "Shiryō bakumatsu ishin no shūmon to kokka." In *Kyōka kenkyū,* vols. 73and 74 (1975): pp. 2-363.

"Shinto o motte shūkyō to nasu wa kōshitsu no kakin taru koto." In *Shūkyō to Kokka: Nihon kindai shisō taikei 5,* edited by Masato Miyaji and Yoshio Yasumaru. Tokyo: Iwanami shoten, 1988.

Suzuki, Shōsan. "Banmin tokuyō." In *Nihon koten bungaku taikei 83,* edited by Yūshō Miyasaka. Tokyo: Iwanami shoten, 1964.

———. "Kana hōgoshū." In *Nihon koten bungaku taikei 83,* edited by Yūshō Miyasaka. Tokyo: Iwanami shoten, 1964.

Takatori, Masao. *Shinto no seiritsu.* Tokyo: Heibonsha, 1979.

Takayanagi, Kōju. *Ashikaga Takauji.* Tokyo: Shunjūsha, 1995.

Takeda, Chōshū. "Kinsei shakai to bukkyō." In *Iwanami kōza nihon rekishi 9: Kinsei,* edited by Saburō Ienaga et al. Tokyo: Iwanami shoten, 1975.

Tayama, Katai. "Jūemon no saigo." In *Kunikita Doppo Tayama Kataishū: Gendai nihon bungaku taikei 11.* Tokyo: Chikuma shobō, 1970.

Tsu Jichinsai Iken Soshō O Mamorukai. *Saikōsai to kamigami.* Tokyo: Shinkyō shuppansha, 1980.

Yanagita, Kunio. "Nihon no matsuri." In *Teihon Yanagita Kunioshū 10.* Tokyo: Chikuma shobō, 1962.

————. "San Sebasuchan." In *Teihon Yanagita Kunioshū 22.* Tokyo: Chikuma shobō, 1962.

————. "Senzo no hanashi." In *Teihon Yanagita Kunioshū 10.* Tokyo: Chikuma shobō, 1962.

————. "Fukō naru geijutsu." In *Teihon Yanagita Kunioshū 7.* Tokyo: Chikuma shobō, 1963.

————. "Heibon to hibon." In *Teihon Yanagita Kunioshū 24.* Tokyo: Chikuma shobō, 1963.

————. "Nenchū gyōji oboegaki." In *Teihon Yanagita Kunioshū 13.* Tokyo: Chikuma shobō, 1963.

————. "Kokyō shichijūnen." In *Teihon Yanagita Kunioshū 3.* Tokyo: Chikuma shobō, 1963.

————. "Yama no jinsei." In *Teihon Yanagita Kunioshū 4.* Tokyo: Chikuma shobō, 1963.

————. *Meiji taishōshi: Sesōhen.* Tokyo: Heibonsha, 1967.

Yō, Eiji. *Chūgoku kinsei no shūkyō rinri to shōnin seishin.* Translated by Noriko Mori. Tokyo: Heibonsha, 1991.

Index

Ama, Toshimaro (The Author): Professor at Meiji Gakuin University in Tokyo. Born in 1939 and graduated from Kyoto University, Japan. In 1962, he started working at NHK (*Nihon Hōsō Kyōkai*, Japan National Broadcasting Station) and later served as a chief program director. His major work is *Zen no sekai* (lit. The World of Zen), a collaborated program among Japanese, French, and German Broadcasting Stations. He has published numerous articles and essays and more than ten book in Japanese.

Ama, Michihiro (The Translator): received a M.A. degree in Buddhist Study from Ōtani University in Kyoto in 1999. Currently he is enrolling in a Ph.D. program at the University of California, Irvine. He is a son of the author.